THE
Mel Bay COMPLETE

STEEL GUITAR
METHOD

by *Roger Filiberto*

PUBLISHER'S NOTE

In all parts of the world the popularity of the Steel is almost unbelievable. Its characteristic charm and tone quality have proven irresistible. People are thrilled and fascinated by the way they can play and express themselves.

Shortly however, they ask this question: "How can I play my favorite tunes with full harmony from the popular song sheets since the music of today is not arranged for this instrument?"

The purpose of this book is to show how this can best be accomplished in a simple direct way, eliminating the arduous study and practice formerly required in the attainment of this style of playing.

Now with the help of this book you can select your favorite or standard song and instantly play it in a full-bodied style on the electric Steel Guitar.

This is a legitimate up-to-date method in the style employed by the top professional artists employing the use of actual pitch. This is the pitch used in the melody line of all popular song sheets.

The E-7th tuning is the tuning used due to the simplicity and ease in the playing of full harmony so vital in the arranging of the current melodies of today.

Mr. Filiberto has successfully used this method for many years and I recommend it as the finest presentation of this type of method ever presented to those desirous of playing the electric Steel Guitar.

Mel Bay

1 2 3 4 5 6 7 8 9 0

AUTHOR'S NOTE

As a student, the author quickly became aware of the lack of material available for the development of playing Melody and Chord style from piano sheet music.

It is with this in mind that the author has made a serious effort to present in as brief and concise a manner, genuine information toward the development of the technique and knowledge necessary in the playing of Melody-Chord style.

No book can replace the instruction that can be provided by a good teacher. Nevertheless, this work will be of great service to teacher and pupil alike; it presents in a systematic manner the necessary basic principles and studies so essential to the beginner student.

With the knowledge that anything worthwhile takes time and effort the author urges the student not to rush through this work. Speed is not the result of haphazard or hurried practice. It is a "by-product" of knowing what to do.

Be patient . . . . . . it takes time to develop the knowledge and skill necessary for playing this beautiful instrument.

                                                        Roger Filiberto

3

THE CORRECT WAY TO HOLD THE STEEL GUITAR

THE STEEL GUITAR
SHOULD REST COMFORTABLY
ON THE LAP. THE FEET SHOULD
BE FIRMLY PLACED SO THAT THE
INSTRUMENT IS IN A LEVEL POSITION.

HOLDING THE BAR

THE BAR POSITION IS USED TO PLAY TWO
OR MORE STRINGS AT THE SAME FRET.

THE STEEL CONTACTS ALL SIX STRINGS
DIRECTLY OVER THE NECESSARY FRET.

THE THIRD AND FOURTH FINGERS REST ON
THE STRINGS IN BACK OF THE STEEL AND
ARE USED FOR "GUARDING" WHEN SHIFTING
FROM POSITION TO ANOTHER. THIS PREVENTS
BUZZING AND HELPS IN THE PRODUCTION OF
THE TONE DESIRED.

4

SLANT POSITION

THIS POSITION IS USED TO
PLAY TWO OR MORE NOTES
AT DIFFERENT FRETS.

REVERSE SLANT POSITION

NOTE THAT THE STEEL IS HELD WITH THE
THUMB AND FINGERS WITH THE THIRD AND
FOURTH FINGERS DOING THE "GUARDING."

THE TILTED STEEL POSITION

THE STEEL IS HELD FIRMLY WITH THE THUMB AND FIRST FINGER
IN THIS MANNER WITH THE REMAINING FINGERS GUARDING
AND CONTROLLING THE POSITION OF THE STEEL.

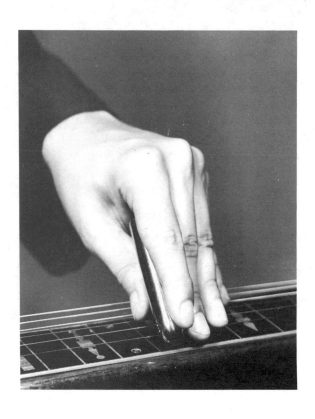

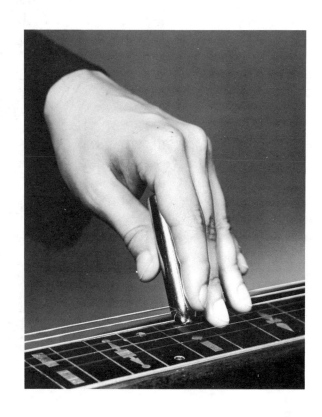

THE RIGHT HAND

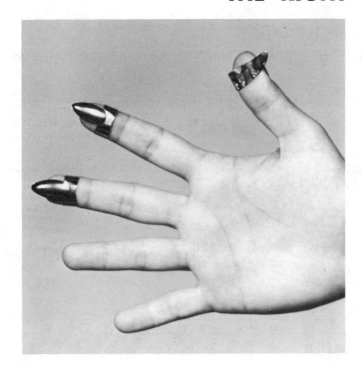

THE RIGHT HAND FINGERS WILL BE DESIGNATED IN THIS MANNER:

T - thumb
. - first finger
. . - second finger

PICKING THE STRINGS

DO NOT "DIG" THE PICKS INTO THE STRINGS BUT GENTLY PLUCK THUS AVOIDING UNNECESSARY NOISES CAUSED BY HARSH PICKING.

HOW TO TUNE THE STEEL GUITAR

THE E 7th TUNING

The names of the six strings on the Steel guitar are B D E G♯ B E — the first string being the highest sounding one.

While the above tuning is recommended for all around playing, the music is arranged so that the sixth string can be lowered to E. This forms the E7th tuning of E D E G♯ B E, which is preferred by some players.

On this page are shown several different methods of tuning — regardless of which method you use, always check the strings over a second time.

TUNING TO A PIANO

A standard piano keyboard has seven and one-third octaves. Middle C is the 24th white key, counting from the left. Tune each string on the Steel guitar so it sounds like the corresponding note on the piano.

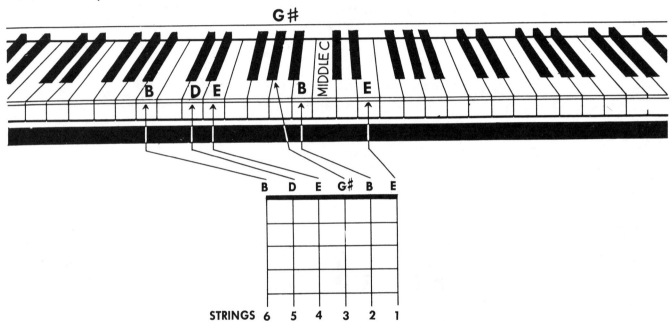

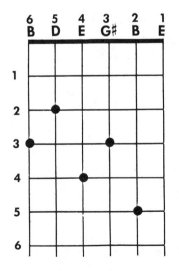

TUNING TO AN "E" PITCH PIPE

Tune the E or first string so that it sounds like the E pitch pipe or tuner.

Then tune each of the other strings by placing the steel over the fret indicated by the black dot and tuning it to sound exactly like the string pictured to the right on the chart.

TUNING TO AN "A" PITCH PIPE

Place the steel over the fifth fret on the first string which produces the tone "A" and tune it so it sounds exactly like the A pitch pipe. Then tune each of the other strings as outlined under "TUNING TO AN 'E' TUNER".

TUNING WITHOUT A PIANO OR PITCH PIPE

Tune the E or first string until you judge it to be at the correct pitch — then tune the balance of the strings as outlined under "TUNING TO AN 'E' TUNER — care should be exercised in not tuning the strings too high as this might cause excessive string breakage.

THE RUDIMENTS OF MUSIC

THE STAFF: Music is written on a STAFF consisting of FIVE LINES and FOUR SPACES. The lines and spaces are numbered upward as shown:

5TH LINE
4TH LINE   4TH SPACE
3RD LINE   3RD SPACE
2ND LINE   2ND SPACE
1ST LINE   1ST SPACE

THE LINES AND SPACES ARE NAMED AFTER LETTERS OF THE ALPHABET.

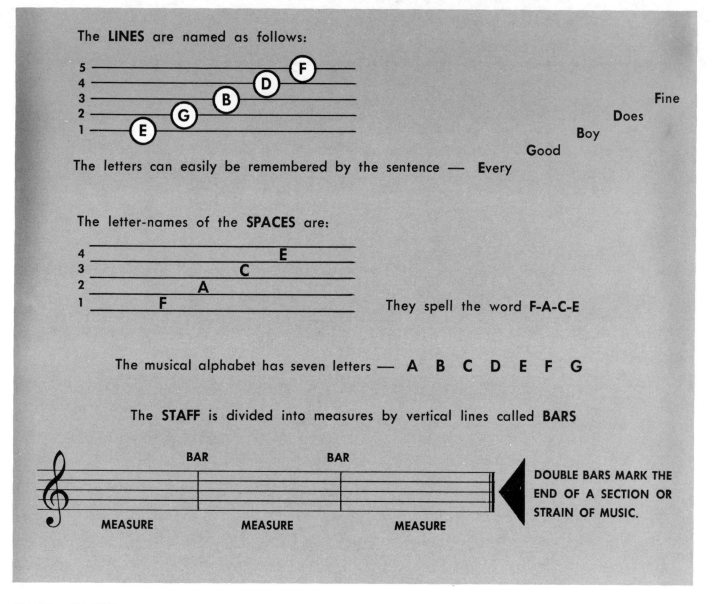

The **LINES** are named as follows:

The letters can easily be remembered by the sentence — Every Good Boy Does Fine

The letter-names of the **SPACES** are:

They spell the word **F-A-C-E**

The musical alphabet has seven letters — **A B C D E F G**

The **STAFF** is divided into measures by vertical lines called **BARS**

BAR   BAR

MEASURE   MEASURE   MEASURE

DOUBLE BARS MARK THE END OF A SECTION OR STRAIN OF MUSIC.

THE CLEF:

THIS SIGN IS THE TREBLE OR G CLEF.

THE SECOND LINE OF THE TREBLE CLEF IS KNOWN AS THE G LINE. MANY PEOPLE CALL THE TREBLE CLEF THE G CLEF BECAUSE IT CIRCLES AROUND THE G LINE.

ALL GUITAR MUSIC WILL BE WRITTEN IN THIS CLEF.

NOTES:

THIS IS A NOTE: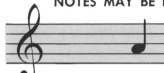

A NOTE HAS THREE PARTS. THEY ARE

The HEAD
The STEM
The FLAG

NOTES MAY BE PLACED IN THE STAFF,   ABOVE THE STAFF,

AND BELOW THE STAFF.

A note will bear the name of the line or space it occupies on the staff.

The location of a note in, above or below the staff will indicate the Pitch.

PITCH: the height or depth of a tone.

TONE: a musical sound.

TYPES OF NOTES

THE TYPE OF NOTE WILL INDICATE THE LENGTH OF ITS SOUND.

THIS IS A WHOLE NOTE. THE HEAD IS HOLLOW. IT DOES NOT HAVE A STEM.

◯ = 4 BEATS
A WHOLE-NOTE WILL RECEIVE FOUR BEATS OR COUNTS.

THIS IS A HALF NOTE THE HEAD IS HOLLOW. IT HAS A STEM.

♩ = 2 BEATS
A HALF-NOTE WILL RECEIVE TWO BEATS OR COUNTS.

THIS IS A QUARTER NOTE THE HEAD IS SOLID. IT HAS A STEM.

♩ = 1 BEAT
A QUARTER NOTE WILL RECEIVE ONE BEAT OR COUNT.

THIS IS AN EIGHTH NOTE THE HEAD IS SOLID. IT HAS A STEM AND A FLAG.

♪ = ½ BEAT
AN EIGHTH-NOTE WILL RECEIVE ONE-HALF BEAT OR COUNT. (2 FOR 1 BEAT)

RESTS:

A REST is a sign used to designate a period of silence.

This period of silence will be of the same duration of time as the note to which it corresponds.

 THIS IS AN EIGHTH REST   { THIS IS A QUARTER REST

 THIS IS A HALF REST. NOTE THAT IT LAYS ON THE LINE.

THIS IS A WHOLE REST. NOTE THAT IT HANGS DOWN FROM THE LINE.

NOTES

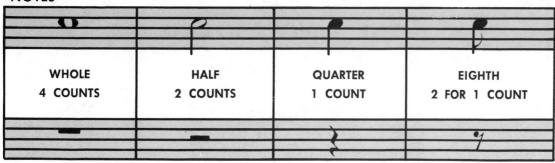

| WHOLE 4 COUNTS | HALF 2 COUNTS | QUARTER 1 COUNT | EIGHTH 2 FOR 1 COUNT |

RESTS

THE TIME SIGNATURE

THE ABOVE EXAMPLES ARE THE COMMON TYPES OF TIME SIGNATURES TO BE USED IN THIS BOOK.

 THE TOP NUMBER INDICATES THE NUMBER OF BEATS PER MEASURE.

THE BOTTOM NUMBER INDICATES THE TYPE OF NOTE RECEIVING ONE BEAT.

 BEATS PER MEASURE

A QUARTER-NOTE RECEIVES ONE BEAT

 SIGNIFIES SO CALLED "COMMON TIME" AND IS SIMPLY ANOTHER WAY OF DESIGNATING $\frac{4}{4}$ TIME.

LEDGER LINES:

When the pitch of a musical sound is below or above the staff, the notes are then placed on, or between, extra lines called LEDGER LINES.

THEY WILL BE LIKE THIS:

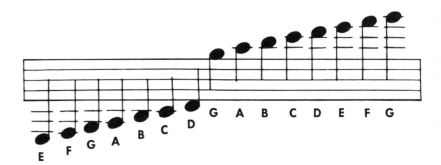

THE FINGERBOARD

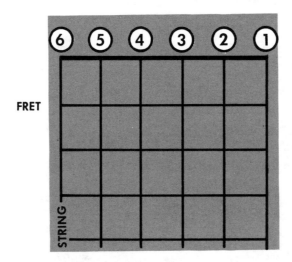

The vertical lines are the STRINGS.

The horizontal lines are the FRETS.

The encircled numbers are the number of the STRINGS.

STRING-NUMBERS: The encircled numbers **6 5 4 3 2 1** will be the numbers of the STRINGS.

CHARTS:

The charts used in this book will have the VERTICAL-LINES as the STRINGS and the HORIZONTAL-LINES as the FRETS.

Reading from left to right the strings will be: ⑥ ⑤ ④ ③ ② ①

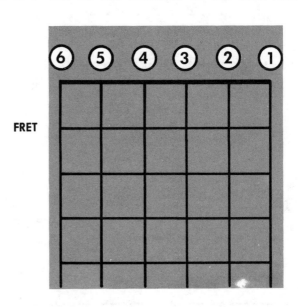

NOTES ON THE E or 1st string

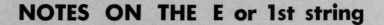

F	Played on the first fret
G	Played on the third fret
A	Played on the fifth fret
B	Played on the seventh fret
C	Played on the eighth fret

Be sure to play all single notes with the tip position

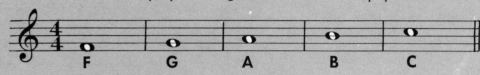

EXERCISE ON WHOLE NOTES: Four counts or beats to each note. Count slowly and evenly. Never play faster than you are capable.

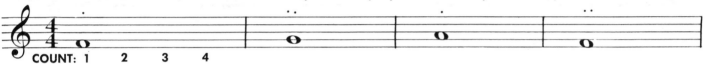

COUNT: 1 2 3 4

EXERCISE ON HALF NOTES: Two counts to each note.

COUNT: 1 2 3 4

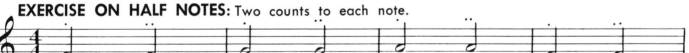

The dots placed above and below the third line of the staff at the double-bar indicate that the exercise is to be repeated.

EXERCISE ON QUARTER NOTES: One count to each note.

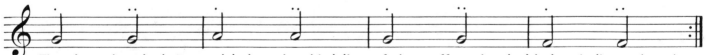

COUNT: 1 2 3 4

QUARTER REST

EXERCISE ON QUARTER AND HALF NOTES.

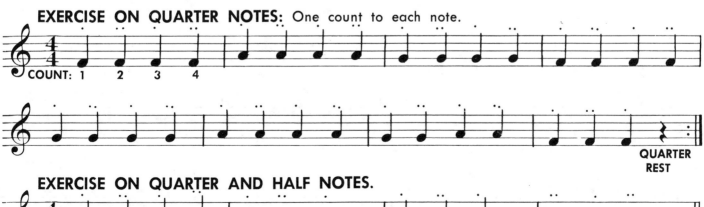

COUNT: 1 2 3 4

12

NOTES ON THE "B" (2nd string)

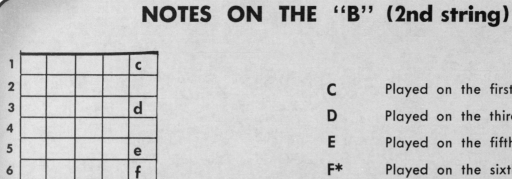

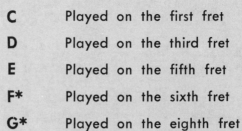

C	Played on the first fret
D	Played on the third fret
E	Played on the fifth fret
F*	Played on the sixth fret
G*	Played on the eighth fret

*F & G are the same F & G as played on the 1st string thereby giving you a choice of which string to play the note on.

Practice these notes on the second string for this lesson.

C D E F G

EXERCISE ON WHOLE NOTES

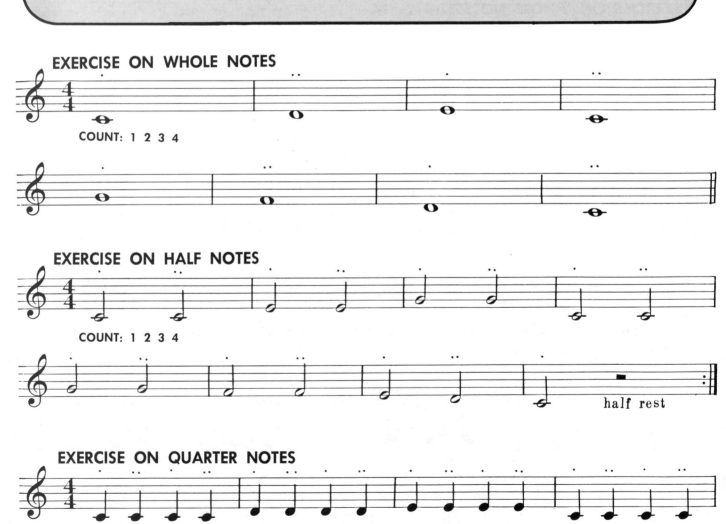

COUNT: 1 2 3 4

EXERCISE ON HALF NOTES

COUNT: 1 2 3 4

half rest

EXERCISE ON QUARTER NOTES

COUNT: 1 2 3 4

INTRODUCING THE DOTTED HALF-NOTE

A DOT (•) placed after a note increases its value by one-half.

A dotted half-note (𝅗𝅥.) will receive three beats.

⚪ Circle indicates string thus ② meaning 2nd string.

Notes not marked will be played on the first string.

COMBINING THE FIRST AND SECOND STRINGS
THE FIRST TUNE   Goodnight Ladies

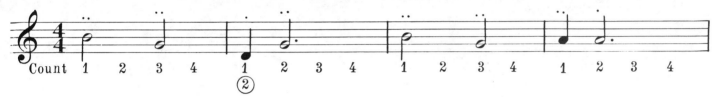

Count   1   2   3   4   1   2   3   4   1   2   3   4   1   2   3   4

Long, Long Ago

Play the following melody using the tip position of the steel throughout.
Reminder: Number in circle below notes indicates string.

STEP BY STEP

Melody for locating single notes — play on the first string unless a number in a circle indicates otherwise.

COUNT: 1 2 3 4

INTRODUCING THREE-FOUR TIME

Indicates THREE-FOUR time.

THIS SIGN: 𝄞 3/4

In THREE-FOUR time, we have three beats per measure.

3 — The number 3 indicates three beats per measure.
4 — The number 4 indicates each quarter note will receive one beat.

The First Waltz

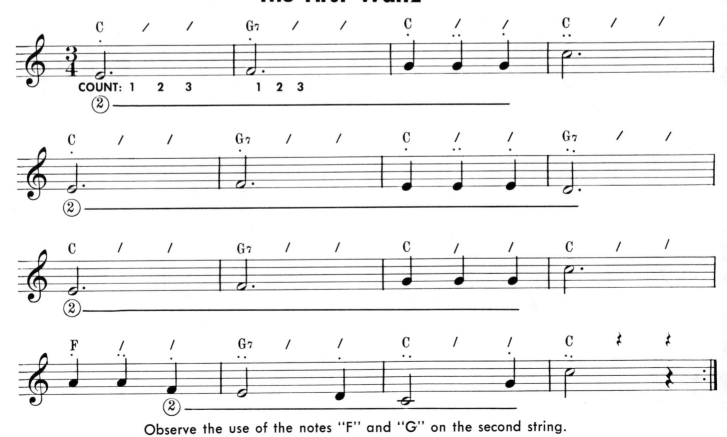

Observe the use of the notes "F" and "G" on the second string.

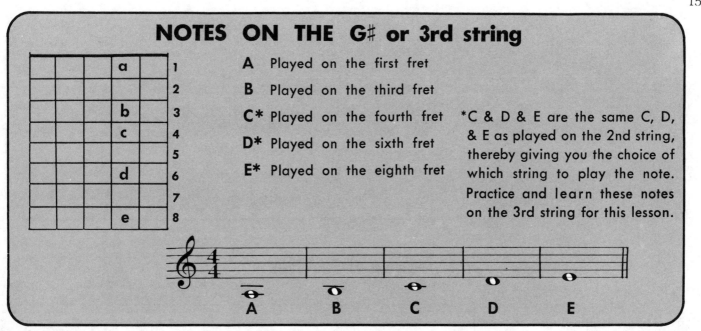

NOTES ON THE G♯ or 3rd string

A Played on the first fret

B Played on the third fret

C* Played on the fourth fret

D* Played on the sixth fret

E* Played on the eighth fret

*C & D & E are the same C, D, & E as played on the 2nd string, thereby giving you the choice of which string to play the note. Practice and learn these notes on the 3rd string for this lesson.

PRACTICE ALL NOTES ON THIS STRING WITH R. H. THUMB

EXERCISE ON WHOLE NOTES

COUNT: 1 2 3 4 T etc.
T

EXERCISE ON HALF NOTES

COUNT: 1 2 3 4 T T etc.
T T

EXERCISE ON QUARTER NOTES

COUNT: 1 2 3 4 etc.
T T T T

NEW TIME SIGNATURE

EXAMPLE

Using the letter C as the time signature is simply an abbreviation for Common Time. Common Time (C) and $\frac{4}{4}$ time are read and played the same.

London Bridge

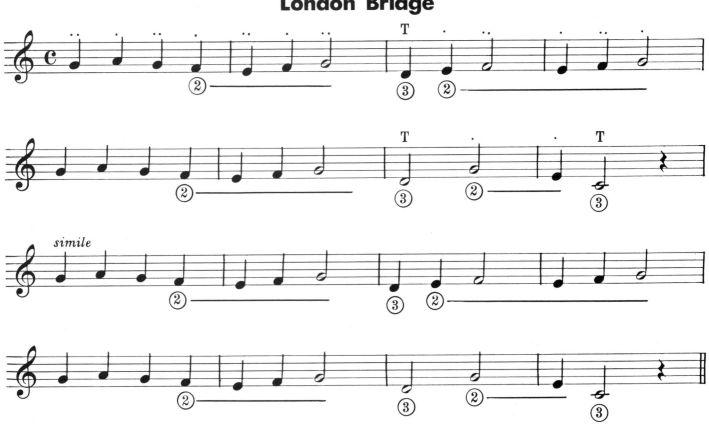

Star Trek

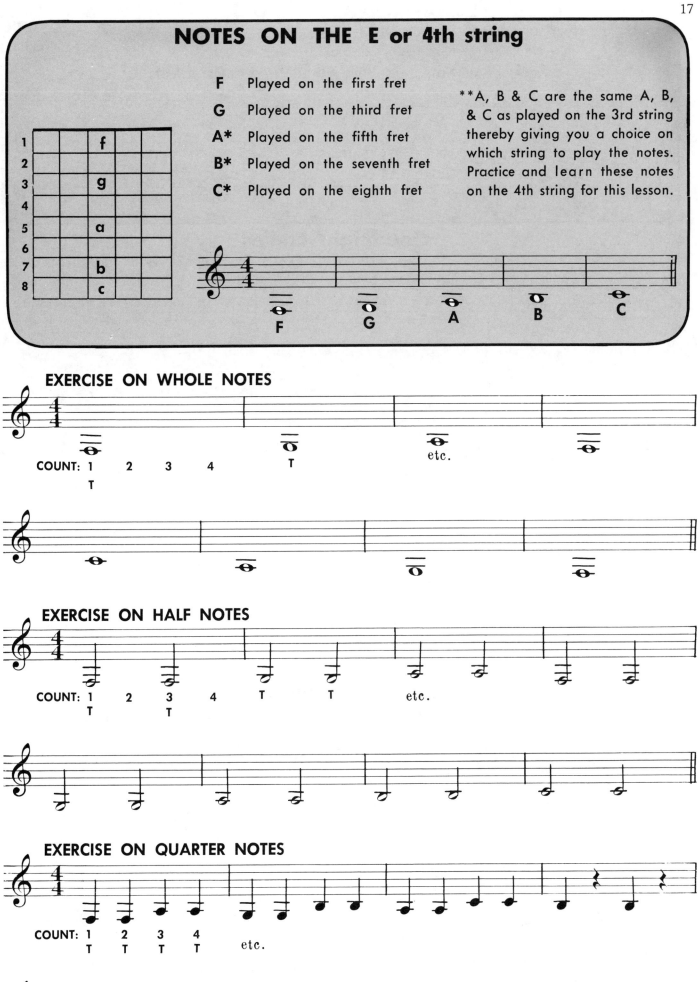

18

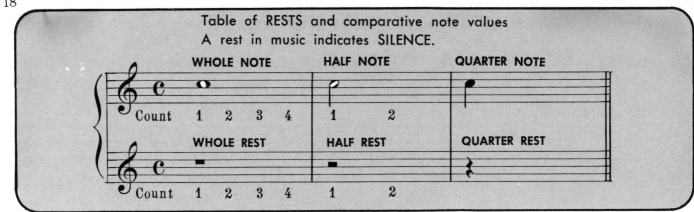

Goodnight Ladies

To silence (or dampen) a note played on the steel guitar, quickly and gently lay the palm of the right hand over the strings. Do not use the palm flatly, but more on the side using the 4th finger (or pinky) as part of the action.

Time Out, Amigo

ADDITIONAL NOTES ON THE E or 1st string

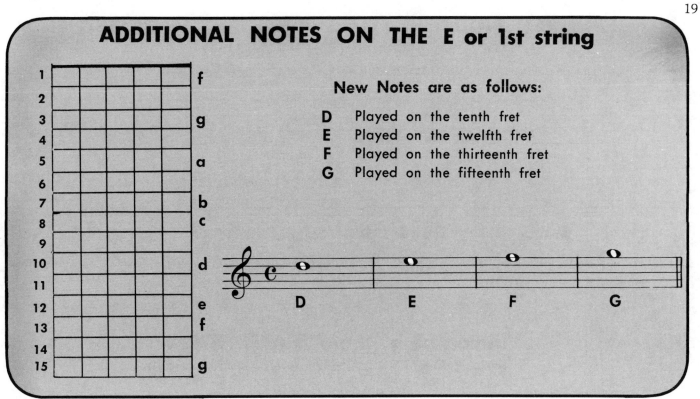

New Notes are as follows:

D Played on the tenth fret
E Played on the twelfth fret
F Played on the thirteenth fret
G Played on the fifteenth fret

Step by Step

Melody for locating single notes — play on the first string unless a number in a circle indicates otherwise.

Letters and following dashes above the staff indicate the chords that can be played on another instrument for accompaniment.

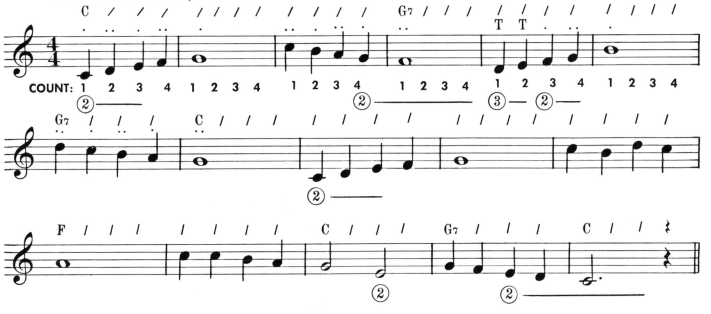

Holiday Waltz

Melody played entirely on the first string.

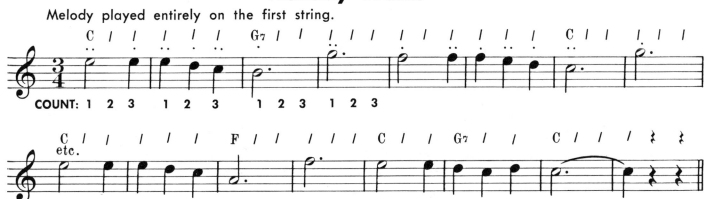

FIRST STUDY PLAYING TWO NOTES TOGETHER
(Observe Fingering Carefully)
This combination of notes is called a "third" *see foot-note

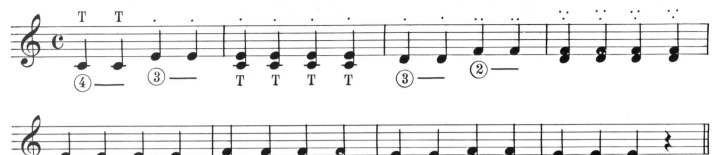

*THIRDS — By "thirds" is meant an interval of three notes. An interval is the distance between two notes. Thus, from C to E is a third because there are three notes from C to E — C, D, and E.

Thirds are easy to recognize as they are written on two adjacent lines one above the other or in two adjacent spaces.

Introducing the "SLANT STEEL"
on the combinations C & A (2nd measure), D & B (3rd measure).

This combination of notes will be called a "sixth" *see foot-note.

This study will be played entirely on the 1st and 3rd strings.

*SIXTHS — By "sixths" is meant an interval of six notes. Thus from B to G is a sixth because there are six notes from B to G — B, C, D, E, F, and G.

Sixths are easy to recognize. One of the notes is in a space and the other one on a line. There are two lines between the two notes.

NEW NOTES ON THE G♯ or 3rd string

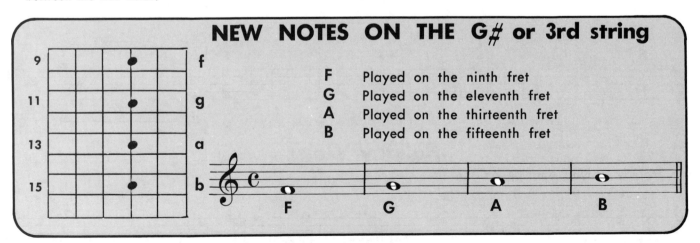

F	Played on the ninth fret
G	Played on the eleventh fret
A	Played on the thirteenth fret
B	Played on the fifteenth fret

THE VIBRATO
The vibrato is a tremolo effect obtained by rapidly alternating the original tone with a slightly preceptible variation in the pitch. On the steel guitar this tone is produced by a rapid back and forth oscillating motion. The third and fourth fingers of the left hand are kept steady on the strings, with the thumb, first and second fingers that hold the bar being the only part that actually moves. Your teacher will help you to develop this fine art.

TIED NOTES

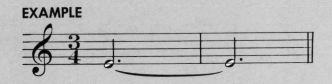

EXAMPLE

A curved line connecting two or more notes on the same line or space is called a tie. In the example above, the first note is tied to the second note. The first note will be played and held for the full time value of both notes.

The Tie Waltz
LESSON ON THE "TIE"
Use the vibrato on all half notes and notes of greater value.

TIED NOTE STUDY IN THREE-QUARTER TIME

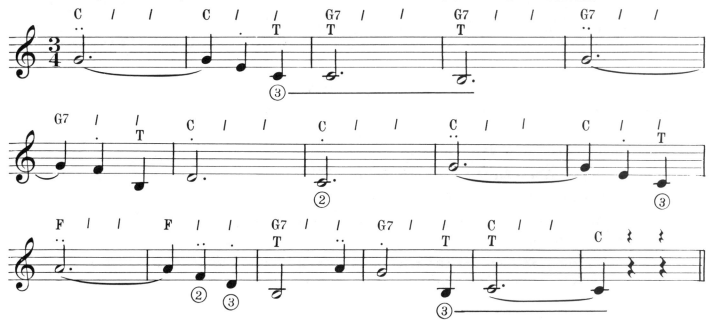

Down In The Valley

Use the vibrato
freely.

More on 6th's

THE KEY OF C

All music studied so far in this book has been in the Key of C.

That means that the notes have been taken from the C Scale (shown at right) and made into melodies.

It is called the C Scale because the first note is C and we proceed through the musical alphabet until C reappears. C-D-E-F-G-A-B-C.

We will cover the subject of keys and scales more thoroughly in the Theory and Harmony Chapters appearing later on in this course.

At present we will deal only with basic fundamentals.

THE C SCALE

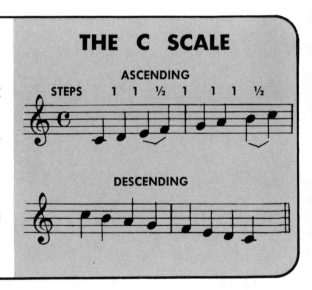

STEPS

A Half-Step is the distance from a given tone to the next higher or lower tone. On the Guitar the distance of a Half-Step is ONE FRET.

A Whole-Step consists of TWO Half-Steps.

The distance of a Whole-Step on the Guitar is TWO FRETS.

The C Scale has two half-steps. They are between E-F and B-C.

Note the distance of one fret between those notes. The distances between C-D, D-E, F-G, G-A, and A-B are Whole-Steps.

Whole-Steps and Half-Steps are also referred to as Whole-Tones and Half-Tones. We will refer to them as Whole-Steps and Half-Steps.

INTRODUCING THE SHARP (#)

A sharp placed in front of a note indicates that the pitch of that note is to be raised one-half tone, or played one fret higher.

EXAMPLE

3RD FRET · 1ST STRING 4TH FRET · 1ST STRING

FIRST AND SECOND ENDING

Sometimes two endings are required in certain selections . . . one to lead back into a repeated chorus and one to close it.
They will be shown like this:

The first time play the bracketed ending **No. 1.** Repeat the tune.

The second time skip the first ending and play ending **No. 2.**

Careless Love

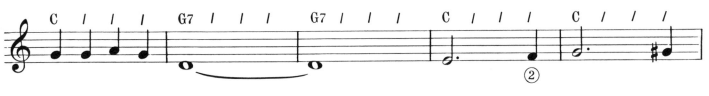

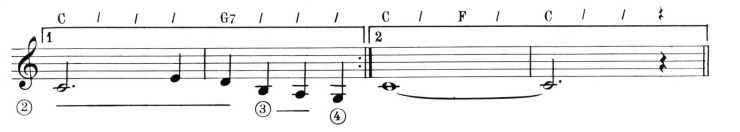

INTRODUCING THE FLAT (♭)

A flat (♭) placed in front of a note indicates that the pitch of that particular note is to be lowered one-half tone, or one fret lower.

EXAMPLE

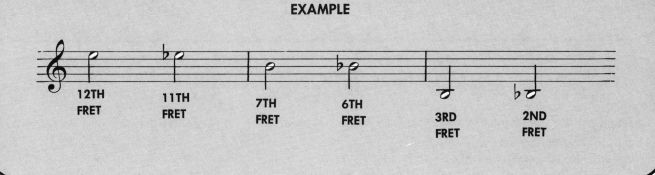

| 12TH FRET | 11TH FRET | 7TH FRET | 6TH FRET | 3RD FRET | 2ND FRET |

Oh Suzanna Boogie

CHROMATICS

The alteration of the pitches of tones is brought about by the use of symbols called CHROMATICS. (Also referred to as ACCIDENTALS)

The Sharp ♯

THE SHARP PLACED BEFORE A NOTE RAISES ITS PITCH ½-STEP OR ONE FRET.

The Flat ♭

THE FLAT PLACED BEFORE A NOTE LOWERS ITS PITCH ½-STEP OR ONE FRET.

The Natural ♮

THE NATURAL RESTORES A NOTE TO ITS NORMAL POSITION. IT CANCELS ALL ACCIDENTALS PREVIOUSLY USED.

"Marching Saints" Boogie
(Rockin Rhythm)

CHART OF THE STEEL GUITAR FINGERBOARD

Showing the names and positions, on the staff and fingerboard, of all notes up to the seventeenth fret

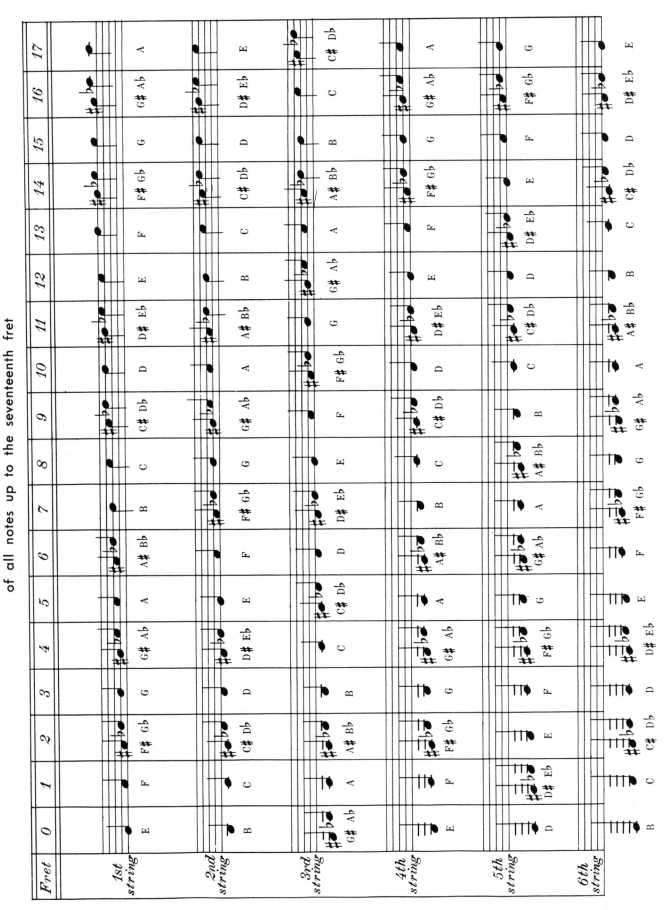

PICK-UP NOTES

All notes written before the first completed measure are referred to as PICK-UP NOTES.

The last measure, plus the PICK-UP NOTES will add up in time value to a completed measure.

Red River Valley

*Remember use the vibrato   A study in pick-up notes and tied-notes.

MORE "DOUBLE NOTE" STUDIES
3rds and 6th's

Play the lower note of all two note combinations with the Right Hand Thumb.

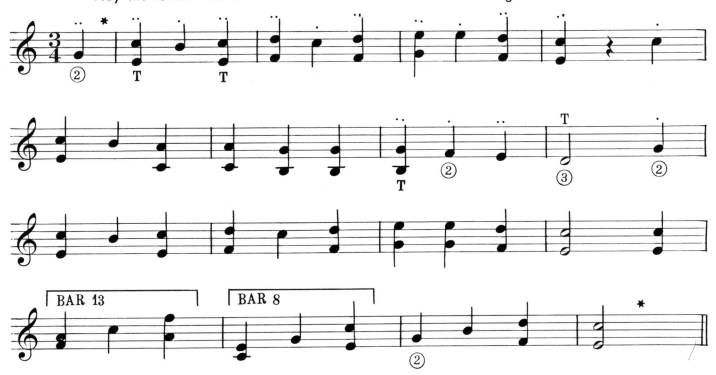

*Observe the pick-up note, and the incomplete measure at the end of this study.

MUSICAL SIGNS, WORDS, PHRASES AND ABBREVIATIONS

Signs, abbreviations and various musical terms are used in popular and standard songs to tell you when to play loud or soft, fast or slow, and to indicate various other musical expressions. The following list shows the most used signs, abbreviations and phases together with their meanings — other words and phases may be found in the dictionary.

SIGNS AND ABBREVIATIONS FREQUENTLY USED

mf — *mezzo-forte* — moderately loud

f — *forte* — — — loud

ff — *fortissimo* — very loud

p — *piano* — — — soft

pp — *pianissimo* — very soft

rit. — *ritardando* — gradually slower

rall. — *rallentando* — gradually slower

accel. — *accelerando* — increase the speed

> — accent sign — to accent or play with emphasis

cresc. — *crescendo* — gradually increase the volume

dim. — *diminuendo* — gradually softer

———— diminuendo sign

———— crescendo sign

⌒ — placed over a note or rest means to hold the note, or rest, longer than its usual time value.

ALPHABETICAL LIST OF MUSICAL WORDS AND PHRASES

Accelerando — Increase the speed

Adagio — Very slow

Ad Libitum (ad lib.) — As you please

Agitato — Restless, agitated

Al Fine — To the end

Alla Breve — (Cut time) — Quick common time

Allegretto — Fairly fast, slower than Allegro but faster than Adante

Allegro — Quick tempo

Andante — Slow movement

Andantino — Faster than Andante

Animato — With life or animation

A Tempo — In tempo

Cadenza — Ornamental passage of music

Coda — A few measures added at the end of compositions

Con Spirito — With spirit and animation

Crescendo — Gradually increase the volume of tone

Da Capo — From the beginning

Da Capo al Fine — From the beginning to the word Fine

Da Capo al Segno — From the beginning to the sign

Dal Segno — From the sign

Decrescendo — To gradually decrease the volume of tone

Diminuendo — To gradually decrease the volume of tone

Divisi — Where two instruments have been playing the same part and then two parts are written with the word Divisi over them, it means that each instrument takes a different part at this point.

Dolce — Sweetly

Dolcissimo — As sweetly as possible

Espressivo — Expressive

Forte — Loud

Fortissimo — Very loud

Glissando — Sliding the steel from one note to another without striking the strings again

Grandioso — Grandly

Larghetto — Broadly — faster than Largo

Largo — Slow, broad tempo

Legato — Smooth, connected

Lento — Slow

Mezzo Forte — Moderately loud

Meno Mosso — With less speed

Moderato — Moderate rate of speed

Pianissimo — Very softly

Piano — Softly

Più Mosso — Faster

Poco a poco — Little by little

Portamento — A slurring together of the sound from one note to another

Prestissimo — Very fast

Presto — Quickly

Ritardando — To retard

Tempo di Marcia — In March time

Tempo di Valse — In Waltz time

Sforzando — With a very strong accent

Vivace — Exceedingly fast

THE EIGHTH NOTE

An eighth note receives one-half beat. (One quarter note equals two eighth notes).

An eighth note will have a head, stem, and flag. If two or more are in successive order they may be connected by a bar. (See Example).

Eighth Notes
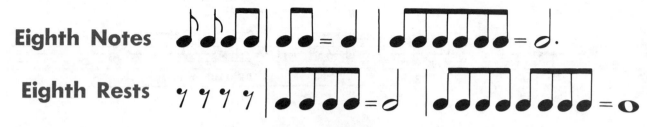

Eighth Rests

The Scale In Eighth Notes

COUNT: 1 & 2 & 3 & 4 &

Little Brown Jug (Study in Eighth Notes)

Count: 1 2 3 & 4   1 2 3 4   1 & 2 3 4   1 2 3 4

1 2 3 & 4   1 2 3 4   1 & 2 & 3 4   1 2 3 4

"Lil Liza" Rock Boogie
(Jive with Liza)

Moderate or
Medium Tempo

Boogie Rock

STUDY IN EIGHTH NOTES

(Tip Position Throughout)

THIRDS IN THE KEY OF C
(Covering a wider range than previously introduced)

The numbers beside the notes indicate the fret over which to place the steel — the thirds with a star below them (*) are played on the third and fourth strings — the others are played on the second and third strings. Practice slowly and name out loud first the lowest and then the highest note of each combination.

Some of the combinations found on the third and fourth strings can also be played with the slant steel on the second and third strings. Example: C and E are found at the bar 8 position on the third and fourth strings and also by slanting the steel at the fifth fret on the second string and the fourth fret on the third string. In determining which combination to play, use the one that sounds smoother and requires less intricate steel handling.

SIXTHS IN THE KEY OF C
(Covering a wider range than previously introduced)

The first combination is played on the second and fourth strings, the next two combinations are on the second and fifth strings, and the rest are all played on the first and third strings — practice slowly and name out loud the lowest and then the highest note of each combination.

Continue to use the vibrato freely.

STUDY IN THREE-FOUR TIME

More "3rd's" in the slant position.

Melody using thirds and sixths — the combinations are all all listed at the top of this page — the two exceptions have numbers beside them to indicate the frets where the notes are played.

Tempo di valse

THE KEY OF A MINOR

(Relative to C Major)

Each Major key will have a Relative Minor key.

The Relative Minor Scale is built upon the **sixth tone** of the Major Scale.

The Key Signature of both will be the same.

The Minor Scale will have the same number of tones (7) as the Major.

The difference between the two scales is the arrangement of the whole-steps and half-steps.

There are **three forms** of the minor scale: **1.** PURE or NATURAL, **2.** HARMONIC, **3.** MELODIC.

THE A MINOR SCALE
Natural (Pure)

HARMONIC

The 7th tone is raised one half-step ascending and descending.

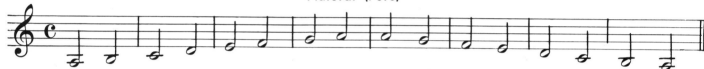

MELODIC

The 6th and 7th tones are raised one half-step ascending and lowered back to their normal pitch descending.

A MINOR MODE

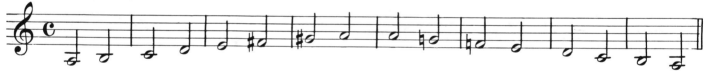

5TH FRET

33

A Daily Scale Study In A Minor

Another Daily Scale Study In A Minor

A Visit To The Relatives

Wildwood Flower
(A Study in Thirds and Sixths)

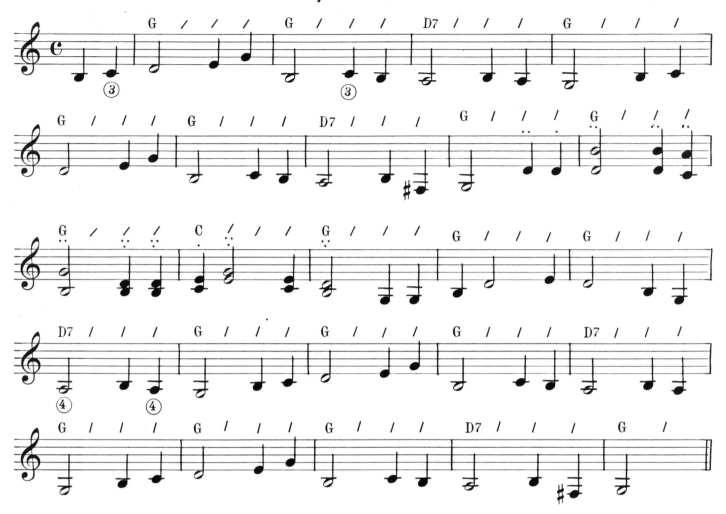

Playtime
(A Study in Sixths)

THE KEY OF G

The Key of **G** will have one sharp. (F♯)

It will be identified by this signature:

The **F-notes** will be played as shown:

THE G SCALE

Note that in order to have the half-steps falling between the seventh and eighth degrees of the scale the F must be sharped.

Our major scale pattern is then correct. (1, 1, ½, 1, 1, 1, ½.) (STEPS)

TWO-FOUR TIME

THIS SIGN INDICATES TWO-FOUR TIME

2 — BEATS PER MEASURE
4 — A QUARTER NOTE RECEIVES ONE BEAT

TWO-FOUR time will have two beats per measure with the quarter note receiving one beat.

Faith Of Our Fathers
All "F's" will be Sharp (♯)

"A Cowboy's Dream"
Using Thirds in the Slant Position
In the Key of "G" All "F's" (#)

Remember! the VIBRATO

*Note that the slant position of the C & E notes at the 4th and 5th frets of the 3rd and 2nd strings is also possible in the bar position at the 8th fret of the 4th and 3rd strings.

THIRDS IN THE KEY OF G

The combinations with stars under them are played on the third and fourth strings — the others are played on the second and third strings — practice slowly naming out loud the two notes in each combination.

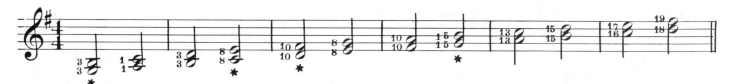

SIXTHS IN THE KEY OF G

The first combination is played on the second and fourth strings — the second combination is played on the second and fifth strings — the balance of the combinations are played on the first and third strings.

Kentucky Moon

Melody using thirds and sixths.   Note the use of accidentals (C#) in the 21st and 22nd measures, and the F♮ in the 16th measure.

Valse Moderato

38

HOW TO READ THE CHARTS

The chart is a section of the guitar fingerboard — the six vertical lines represent the strings and the horizontal lines represent the frets — the vertical line farthest to the left is the 6th or lowest sounding string.

The number at the left of the chart indicates the number of that fret and the black dots show where to place the steel which strings to pick.

CHART 1 — Bar over third fret and pick only the 2nd, 3rd & 4th strings.

CHART 2 — Bar over third fret and pick the first three strings.

CHART 3 — Slant steel for 7th fret on first string and 6th fret on third string — pick only the first and 3rd strings.

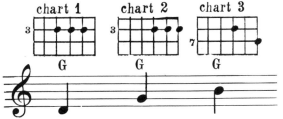

HOW TO PLAY MELODY CHORDS

First, you notice the name of the chord, which in the first measure in the example below is C, and then the name of the melody note, which in the first measure is E — this tells you that you want a C chord with an E as the melody or top note. In the second measure the chord is still C — but the melody or top note changes to G — in the third measure we still retain the C chord but the melody note changes to C and etc. Study the charts below and then proceed to the First study in Harmonizing.

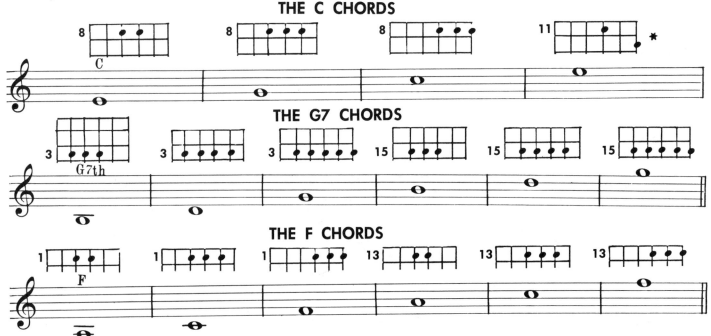

*Slant the steel — pick with thumb and second finger.
When using chord combinations of four or more notes play them with the Right Hand Thumb.

FIRST STUDY IN MELODY CHORDS

Refer to the above listed chord charts as long as necessary. In due time you will memorize the positions.

Use the harmony (chord symbol) indicated over the notes until a new chord symbol is shown — the first three notes are harmonized with the C chord — the three notes in the second measure with the F chord, the next three notes (third measure) with the G7 chord, and so on.

Pick the first and third strings together with the thumb and second finger — pick the third and fourth strings with the thumb and first finger and pick the three string combinations with the thumb, first and second fingers.

SECOND STUDY IN MELODY CHORDS

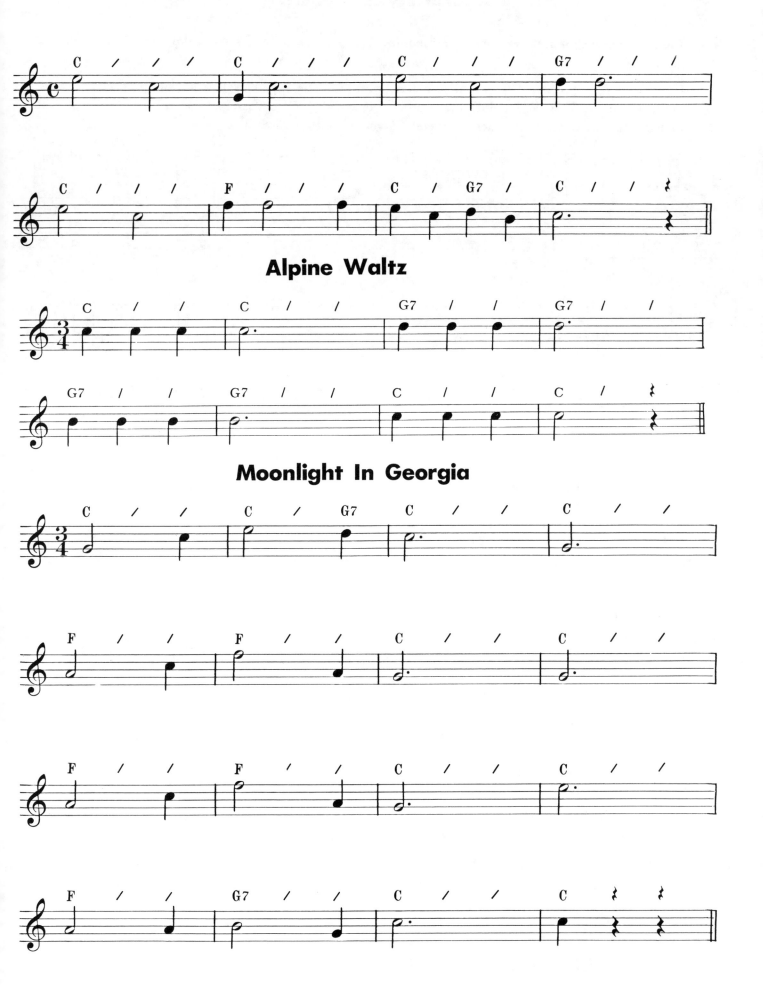

Alpine Waltz

Moonlight In Georgia

MELODY CHORDS IN THE KEY OF "G" (All F's #)
REFERENCE CHARTS

The following charts show how to harmonize the melody notes used in the two studies on this page.

Listed under the G chord, you will find the note "B"* on the third line harmonized at two positions — use the first way unless the note marked with the number three in a circle which means to use the formation that places the melody note on the third string.

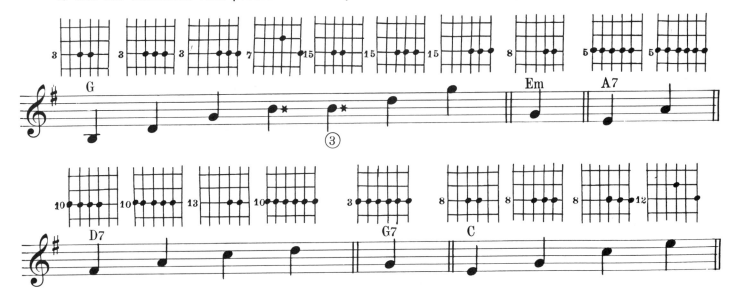

STUDY IN HARMONIZING

Refer to the above charts when harmonizing the following melody notes.

WALTZ SONG

Do not try to harmonize every note—progressions are smoother and more musical if certain notes are played singly.

Harmonize all the melody notes in the following tune with the exception of the four with a check mark over them (√) — these are to be picked singly.

When playing single notes use the tip position of the steel — all four single notes are played on the first string.

A STUDY IN MELODY CHORDS

(Refer to chord diagrams on previous page)

Home On The Range

Pick all eighth notes singly as well as any other notes not found on chord diagram page.

DOTTED QUARTER NOTES

A DOT AFTER A NOTE increases its Value by ONE-HALF.

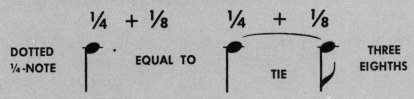

The count for the dotted quarter-note is as follows:

COUNT: 1 2 & 3 4 &   1 2 & 3 4 &   1 2 & 3 4 &   1 2 & 3 4 &

A Dotted Quarter-Note Etude

COUNT: 1 2 &3 4 & 1 2 &3 4&

My Old Kentucky Home

Introducing the dotted quarter note.

Play all single notes in tip position.

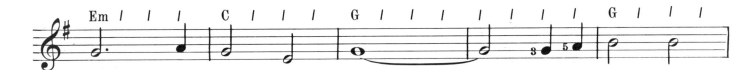

COUNT: 1 2   & 3   4

PLAYING FROM PIANO MUSIC

The example at the left shows how a popular song is written – the top line is the melody and voice part – the second and third lines are played by the piano – the chord names above the melody indicate the harmony and can be followed by any chord instrument for accompaniment purposes.

Many players can read the single note melody or follow the chord name and play accompaniment – but instead of playing a monotonous single note melody, you are going to play the melody in full harmony by associating the chord names with each melody note.

HOW TO FIND THE CHORDS FOR HARMONIZING

You will be given the necessary chords for each lesson. In the following section of this course you will find a complete series of chord charts for every practical chord that can be played.

To find other chords use the following section and look under the chord name indicated – find the melody note to be played – the chart above it shows exactly where to place the steel and which string to pick to harmonize the melody.

DIFFERENT TYPES OF CHORDS

In music there are several different types of chords such as **MAJOR, MINOR, SEVENTH, DIMINISHED, AUGMENTED**, and others – for a complete list see the following section. Major chords are indicated with capital letters such as C, F, G. Minor chords are indicated with a small letter following the name of the chord such as Cm, Fm, Gm. Seventh chords are indicated thus C7, F7, G7. Diminished chords are indicated with the abbreviation "dim." such as C dim., F dim., G dim. Augmented chords are indicated with the plus sign (+) such as C+, F+, G+.

WALTZING WITH YOU

Play the following melody in full harmony – the chart above each note shows where to place the steel and which strings to pick. Pick four or more strings with the thumb – pick three strings together with the thumb, first and second fingers – pick the second and third strings together with the thumb and first finger.

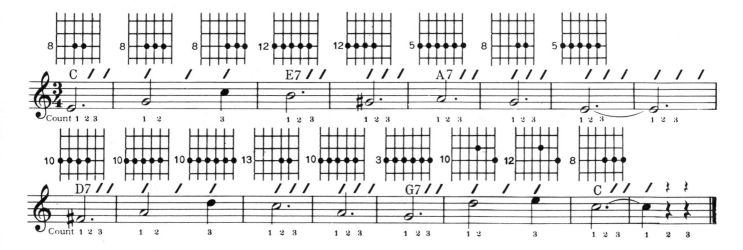

HARMONIZING WITH "THIRDS AND SIXTHS"

When harmonizing songs, follow the top line of the piano part and be on the lookout for series of two note chords written in "thirds" or "sixths" — these can be played exactly as written without the necessity of associating the chord with the melody note.

THIRDS

An interval is the distance between two notes. By "thirds" is meant an interval of three notes. Thus from C to E is a third because there are three notes from C to E — C, D, and E. (See Page Twenty)

Series of thirds are easy to recognize as they are written on two adjacent lines one above the other or in two adjacent spaces.

The example of piano music at the left shows that the seven "two note" chords are written as thirds — these can be read and played exactly as written.

The following pages will be taken up with the study of thirds and sixths in the most used keys — actual piano arrangements are illustrated thus giving you practical experience in reading from piano music.

SIXTHS

By "sixths" is meant an interval of six notes. Thus from C to A is a "sixth" because there are six notes from C to A — C, D, E, F, G and A. (See Page Twenty)

With a little study you will soon learn to recognize series of sixths. One of the notes is in a space and the other one on a line — there are two lines between the two notes.

The example of piano music at the left shows five two note chords written in sixths — study the combinations carefully.

It will be an advantage to read and play thirds and sixths exactly as written — they harmonize perfectly — relieve the monotony of single note and full harmony playing — thus making for a more varied, smooth progressing arrangement.

Seeing Nellie Home
(The Quilting Party)

This melody is arranged for piano and gives a practical example of reading from sheet music. Follow the top line of the piano part — the sequences of notes that are encircled are to be read and played as thirds and sixths, exactly as written — a few of the encircled combinations are three note chords, play the lowest and highest notes only which form a sixth combination—the balance of the melody notes are to be harmonized with the chords indicated. To find melody chord combinations refer to page 38.

*Use only the two note combination with the "x's" as they form a sixth.

REFERENCE CHARTS

Showing how to harmonize the melody notes used on the next page.

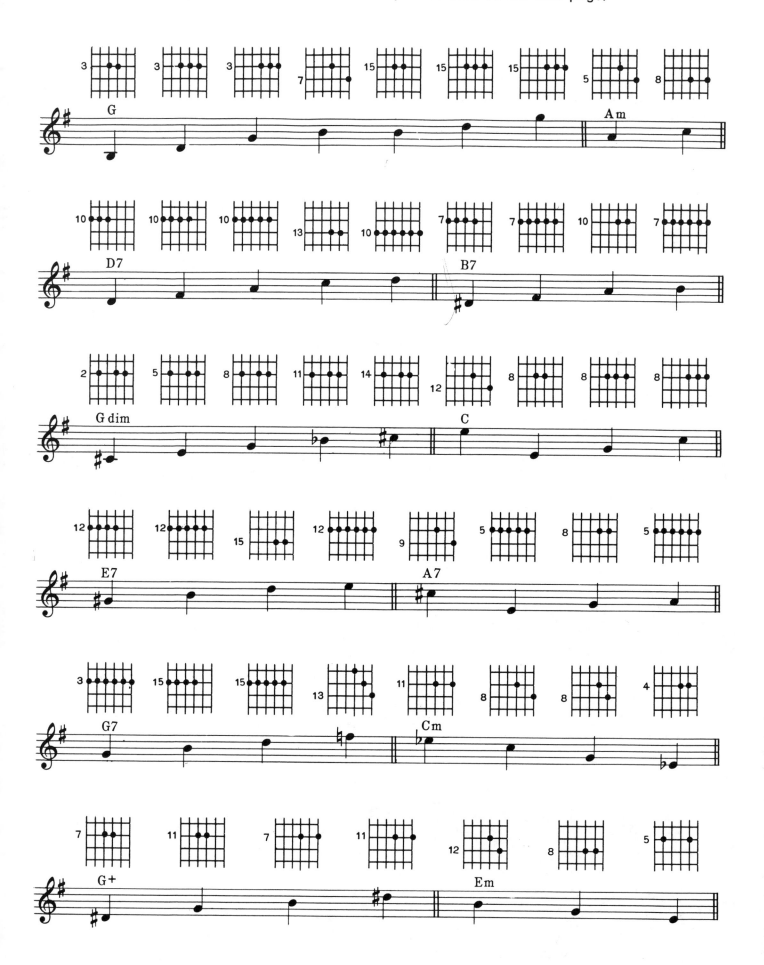

FIRST MODULATION IN G

The charts on the preceding page show how to harmonize the melody notes on this page — two
ways of harmonizing the note B, on the third line, with the G chord are shown; use the first chart
unless the number three in a circle tells you to use the formation that places the melody note on
the third string.

SECOND MODULATION IN G

Harmonize each melody note.

Drifting Clouds

Harmonize each melody note except those indicated with a check mark which are picked singly.

You're In My Dreams

Play the encircled notes as thirds and sixths, exactly as written — pick singly the few notes indicated with a check mark (√) — harmonize the other melody notes with the chords indicated. The numbers beside a few of the notes indicate the frets where steel is to be placed.

A page of rhythm studies

How To Count Triplets

Q. What are TRIPLETS?

A. A group of three notes, played in the time of two notes of the same kind.

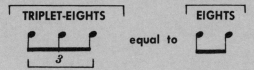

SIXTEENTH-NOTES

In common time four sixteenth-notes equal one quarter-note.

They may be counted in this manner:

1-six-teenth-notes, 2-six-teenth-notes, 3-six-teenth-notes, 4-six-teenth-notes.

Example

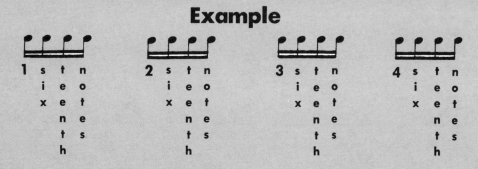

THE DOTTED EIGHTH NOTE

A Dotted Eighth-note is equal to

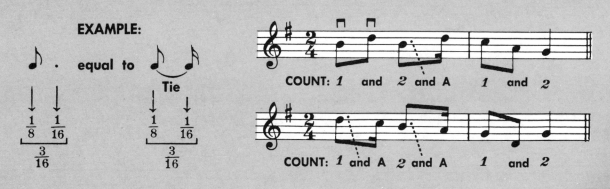

THE KEY OF F MAJOR
REFERENCE CHARTS

Showing how to harmonize the melody notes on the following page

First Modulation in the Key of F

The charts on the preceding page show how to harmonize the following melody notes.

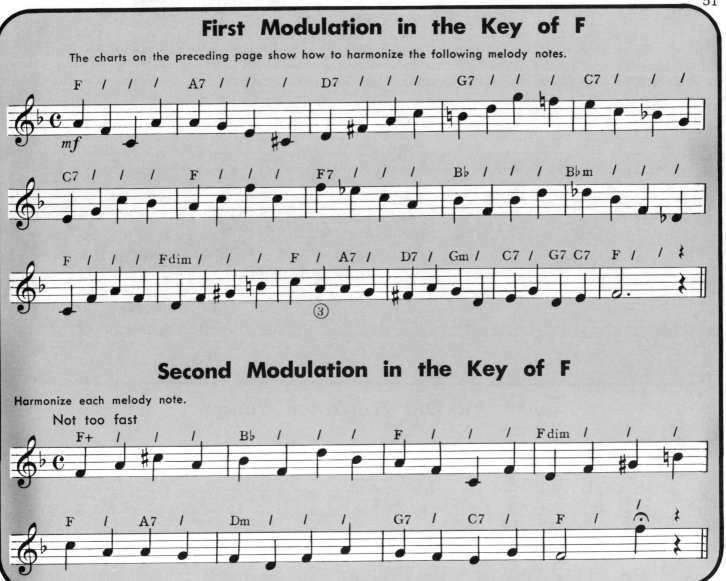

Second Modulation in the Key of F

Harmonize each melody note.

Not too fast

When Soft Shadows Fall

Harmonize each melody note.

Tenderly

52

THIRDS IN THE KEY OF F

The combinations with the stars under them are played on the third and fourth strings — the others are played on the second and third strings. Remember that most of the combinations on the third and fourth strings can also be played three frets lower on the second and third strings, using the slant position.

SIXTHS IN THE KEY OF F

All played on the first and third strings — remember that the one fret slants on the first and third strings, can also be played five frets higher on the second and fifth strings using the bar position.

Just An Old Fashioned Song

Melody using thirds and sixths
Slowly with expression

When You And I Were Young Maggie

Play the encircled thirds and sixths exactly as written — pick the checked notes singly — harmonize all other notes with the chords indicated. Eight strokes to the measure are added in the chord accompaniment to provide a more rhythmic background.

54

THE KEY OF B♭
REFERENCE CHARTS
Showing how to harmonize the melody notes used on the next page.

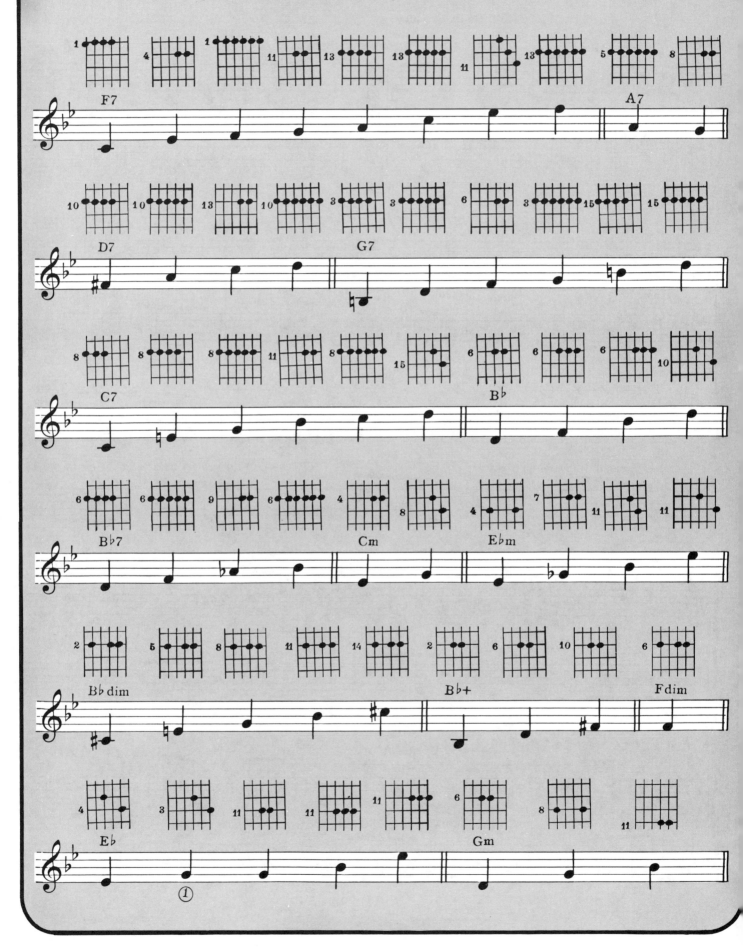

First Modulation in B♭

The charts on the preceding page show how to harmonize the following melody notes — listen as you play — strive to make each chord sound full and resonant — use the VIBRATO freely.

Notice that as you study each new key many of the combinations repeat themselves — you find yourself referring to the charts less and less frequently.

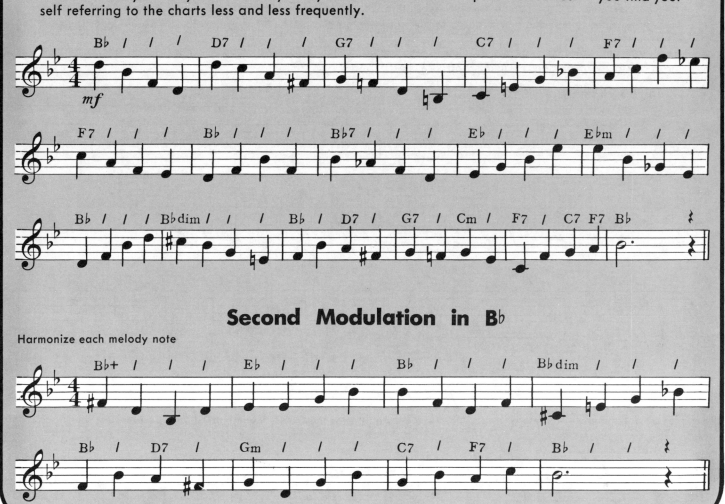

Second Modulation in B♭

Harmonize each melody note

Moonlit Bay

Harmonize each melody note

56

Stepping Along

Pick all notes singly — use the tip position of the steel unless the bar position is indicated.

SINGLE NOTE TECHNIQUE When playing from piano music, bear in mind that it is not necessary to harmonize every melody note — many passages will be picked singly — certain series of thirds and sixths will be played exactly as written — notes of longer duration like whole notes, dotted half notes, half notes, and occasionally dotted quarter and quarter notes will be harmonized by associating the melody note with the chord — it is even advisable at times to play notes of longer duration singly; a lot depends on the character and speed of the individual selection.

This page and the next page are devoted to single note technique and to various types of rhythmic patterns — practice slowly at first and gradually increase the tempo.

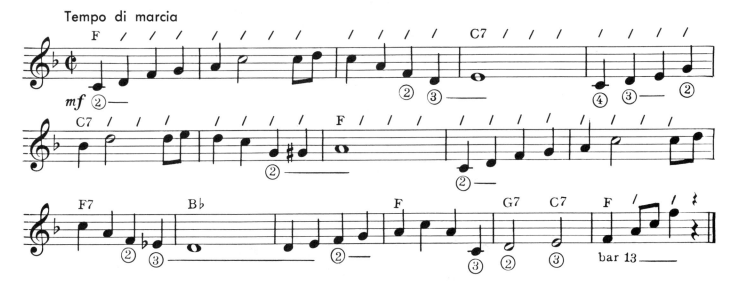

Dreamy Paradise

Pick all notes singly — carefully analyze the rhythmic patterns as they are frequently used in three-four time selections.

Rhythm of the Waves
Study in Single Note Picking

The following tune affords excellent practice in picking melody notes singly — use the tip position of the steel except where the bar position is indicated.

Where certain combinations of notes are repeated, no bar position or string numbers are marked. Refer to the marked sections whenever necessary. As an example: all the notes in the first measure of the first, third, and seventh lines are played with the bar 8 position of the steel.

58

THIRDS IN THE KEY OF B♭

SIXTHS IN THE KEY OF B♭

Savannah Bay

Melody using thirds & sixths

With marked rhythm

Rock of Ages

Play the entire selection using thirds and sixths — where some of the combinations are written as three note chords pick out two notes that make up a sixth.

THE KEY OF E♭
REFERENCE CHARTS
Showing how to harmonize the melody notes used on the next page

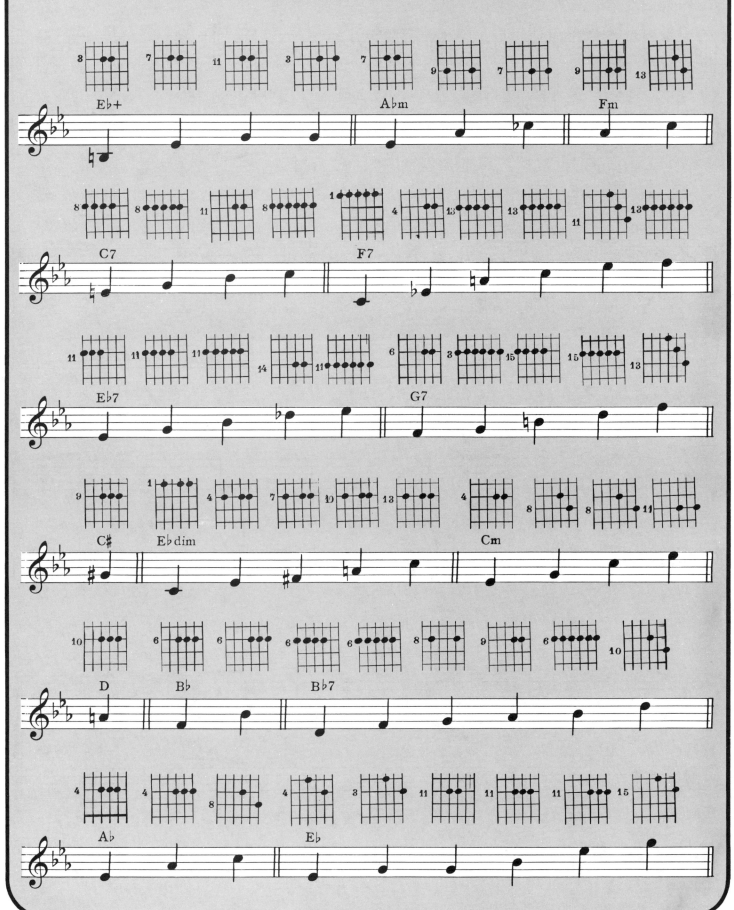

First Modulation in E♭

The charts on the preceding page show how to harmonize each of the following melody notes. Practice slowly — visualize the name of the chord and the name of each melody note as you play.

Second Modulation in E♭

Harmonize each melody note

Fireside Dreams

Harmonize each melody note

Expressivo

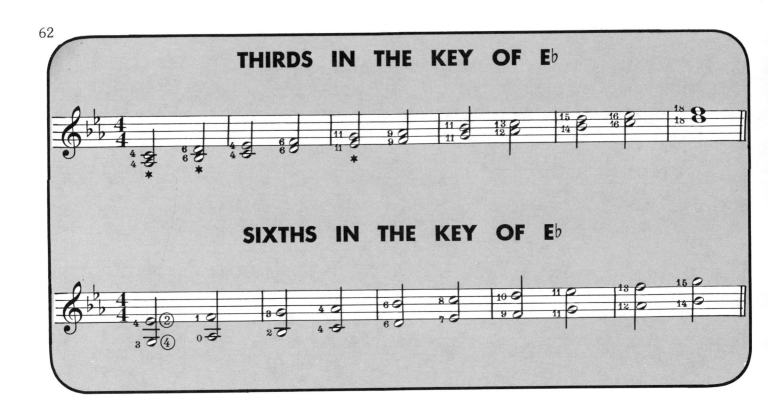

Johnnie's Song

Juanita

In this tune many of the "sixth" combinations are played on the second and fifth strings — the numbers beside the notes indicate the frets over which to place the steel. The encircled notes are played as thirds and sixths — the two checkered notes are picked singly — harmonize all other notes with the chords indicated.

THE KEY OF A♭
REFERENCE CHARTS
Showing how to harmonize the melody notes used on the next page

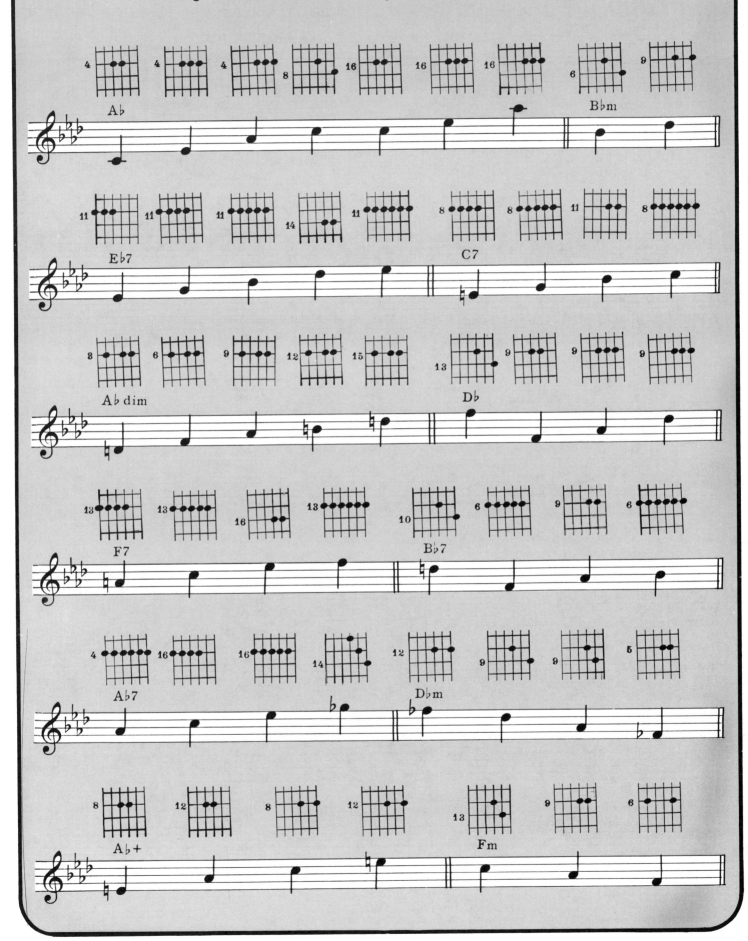

First Modulation in A♭

The charts on the previous page show how to harmonize each of the following melody notes.

Second Modulation in A♭

Harmonize each melody note.

Tennessee Moonlight

Harmonize each melody note.

Andante

66

THIRDS IN THE KEY OF A♭

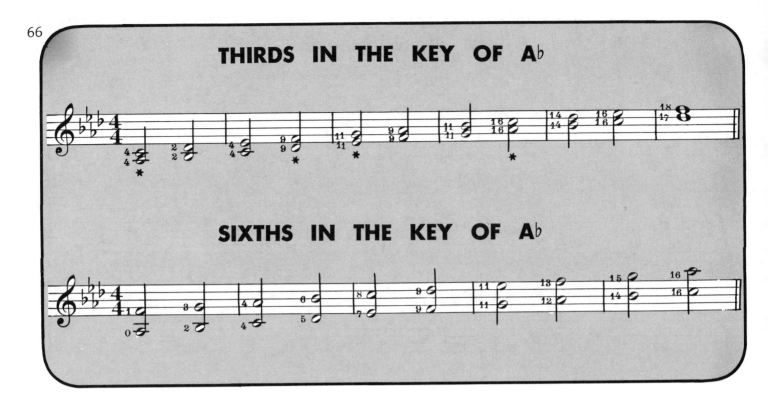

SIXTHS IN THE KEY OF A♭

Steelin' A March

Melody using thirds & sixths

March tempo

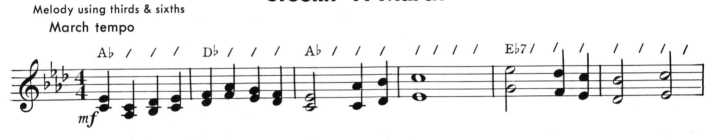

Sweetheart, You and I

Play the encircled notes as thirds and sixths — pick singly the notes indicated with a check mark — harmonize all other notes with the chords indicated.

Teasing the Strings

A study in single note technique and steel handling — use the tip position of the steel except where the bar position is indicated.

Brightly but not too fast

Syncopated Rhythms

Play the notes exactly as written — The melody is harmonized only at the various places where harmony notes are added.

Swing it

CHARACTERISTIC EFFECTS OF STEEL GUITAR

The steel guitar adapts itself readily to certain characteristic effects that can be used in music (even when they are not indicated) to add variety, more expression and a greater range of interpretation.

GRACE NOTES are quickly played notes printed in small type and placed before the regular or principal notes — they borrow their time value from the preceding count, being played a fraction of an instant before the principal notes — grace notes can be added by the player in a number of interesting ways either to single notes or chords:

1. By picking the strings one fret lower than the principal notes and immediately sliding the steel to the principal notes without picking the strings again. (See first measure in the following example.)

2. Double grace notes can be added by picking the principal note as the first grace note and immediately sliding the steel one fret lower and then back to the principal note without picking the strings again. (See sixth measure.)

3. Double grace notes can be added by picking the principal note as the first grace note and immediately sliding the steel one or two frets higher and then back to the principal note without picking the strings again. (See second measure.)

4. Single grace notes can be added on a lower string than the principal note — single grace notes can also be added on a higher string than the principal note. In these cases place the steel for both notes at the same time, whenever possible, but pick the notes separately. (See third and seventh measures.)

Grace notes can be added in many other ways, each way producing a new and different effect.

The **HULA PICK** and **ARPEGGIO** or **HARP STYLE** of playing are in reality two more interesting ways of adding grace notes.

The **HULA PICK** can be used when playing two note chords in slower tunes — the lower note being picked a fraction of an instant before the higher one as though it were as a grace note. Use the hula pick on the two note chords in the following study.

The **ARPEGGIO** or **HARP STYLE** of playing is indicated with a wavy line — it means to pick the strings separately and quite rapidly from the lowest to the highest as though all the notes but the melody were written as grace notes.

The **TREMOLO** can be frequently used when playing two note chords; especially on the first and third strings. The effect is produced by rapid, alternate picking of the two notes starting with the lower one.

The example at the left shows the effect desired. Do not attempt to count the number of notes played — merely follow the tempo and rapidly alternate the picking for the time duration of the notes.

Keep the fingers of the right hand relaxed — strive to make the tremolo sound smooth and continuous. Use the thumb to pick the lower note and either the first or second finger to pick the higher one. The abbreviation "*tr*" is used to indicate the tremolo. In the following study interrupt the tremolo between each group of slurred notes. Do not interrupt the tremolo when changing from one chord to another within a slurred group.

Falling Leaves

Melody using grace notes — play the notes exactly as written — use the tip position of the steel on single notes unless the bar position is indicated.

Waltz Ballard Tempo

Pickin' the Blues

A study in the use of the tremolo — play the notes exactly as written.

Smoothly

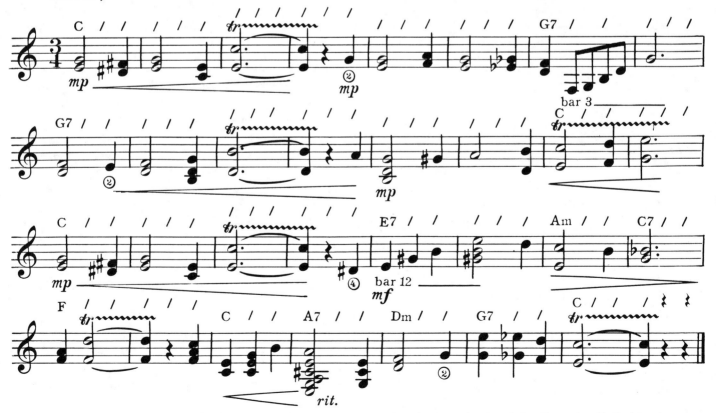

FINGER HARMONICS

FINGER HARMONICS

One of the outstanding features of the steel guitar is the easy, spontaneous response of harmonic tones — these clear, bell-like over-tones produce a tone color that have made the steel guitar, and especially the Electric Steel Guitar, so valuable in modern orchestras.

By using **FINGER** and **PALM HARMONICS**, it is possible to play any note of the scale with this new and different type of tone which adds a great deal of variety to advanced arrangements.

The example at the left shows the position of the right hand when playing FINGER HARMONICS. The steel is placed as usual for the note to be played — then the tip of the third finger of the right hand is extended to lightly contact the string to be played twelve frets higher than the fret on which the steel is placed — then, immediately after the string is picked with the thumb, the third finger is released to allow the harmonic tone to ring clearly. Notice that the thumb picks the string in back of the third finger, toward the bridge — a short decisive stroke of the thumb is used to produce the desired effect.

STUDY USING FINGER HARMONICS

Pick the chord at the beginning of each measure with the thumb — then, while the steel remains at the bar position indicated, play the single notes in each measure using finger harmonics. Diamond shaped notes are used to indicate harmonic tones and the letters F.H. as an abbreviation for FINGER HARMONICS. Notice from their position on the staff that the notes to be played with finger harmonics sound an octave higher than the notes over which the steel is placed.

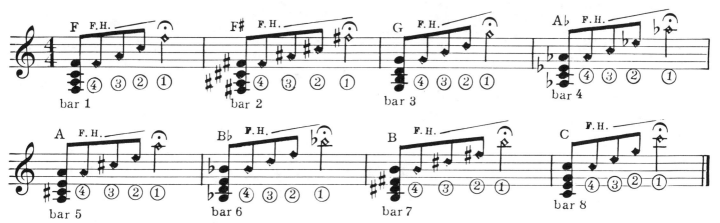

SECOND STUDY IN FINGER HARMONICS

Finger harmonics can also be produced at other positions in addition to those twelve frets than where the steel is placed. By playing them five frets higher, the resultant tone is two octaves higher than the tone produced where the steel is placed. By playing them seven frets higher, the resultant tone is one octave higher than the fret over which the finger of the right hand is extended.

In the following study play the finger harmonics twelve frets higher than where the steel is placed, unless a number over the note indicates some other fret — the notes written indicate the actual tones produced.

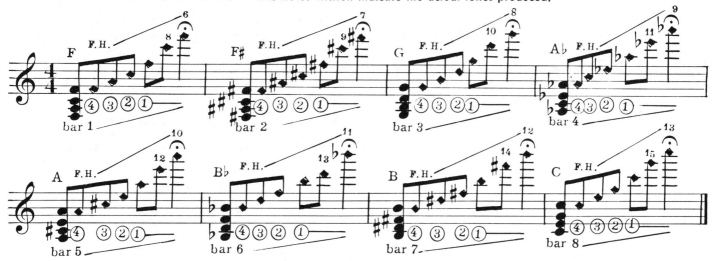

Together Again

Melody using grace notes and finger harmonics — play the notes exactly as written — play the finger harmonics twelve frets higher than where the steel is placed unless a number over the note indicates a different fret for the third finger to contact the string, as in measure fifteen and sixteen.

THE PORTAMENTO

PORTAMENTO means to carry the tone from one note to another by sliding the steel on the string. An unusual and interesting effect can be produced by using the portamento to connect two notes on different strings — pick the first note and slide the steel on the string toward the fret on which the next note is to be played, then immediately shift the steel to the next note and pick it with a slight accent. The slide on the string is executed during the time value of the first note. The whole effect must sound smooth and connected. As soon as the second note is picked the tone from the previous note must be stopped in order to produce the desired effect.

In the following melody the portamento is indicated by a wavy line connecting the notes (〰〰).

Palm Harmonics

PALM HARMONICS are produced by contacting the strings twelve frets higher than where the steel is placed with the edge of the right hand palm on the little finger side — the thumb of the right hand strikes the strings at a point ahead of the hand, toward the peghead.

With palm harmonics it is possible to produce harmonic tones on two or more strings simultaneously as well as on single notes. Palm harmonics have a soft mellow quality of tone as compared to the more brilliant sound of finger harmonics.

Palm contacting the strings for palm harmonics.

Natural playing position of the right hand for playing palm harmonics.

STUDY IN PALM HARMONICS

Use palm harmonics throughout

SECOND STUDY IN PALM HARMONICS

After playing a note with palm or finger harmonics, the harmonic tone can be carried along by sliding the steel to any other fret. It will prove especially to slide the steel an octave (twelve frets) higher after picking the harmonic tone as in the following study.

The term *8va* is an abbreviation for octave and means that the notes should be written an octave higher — to do so however would place them so high above the staff as to make them difficult to read — thus they are written an octave lower than they actually sound with the term *8va* over them to indicate the effect desired.

The letters P.H. are used as an abbreviation for PALM HARMONICS.

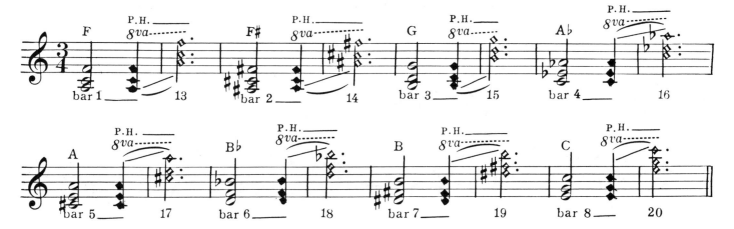

Chimes Waltz

Melody using palm harmonics, finger harmonics and the tremolo

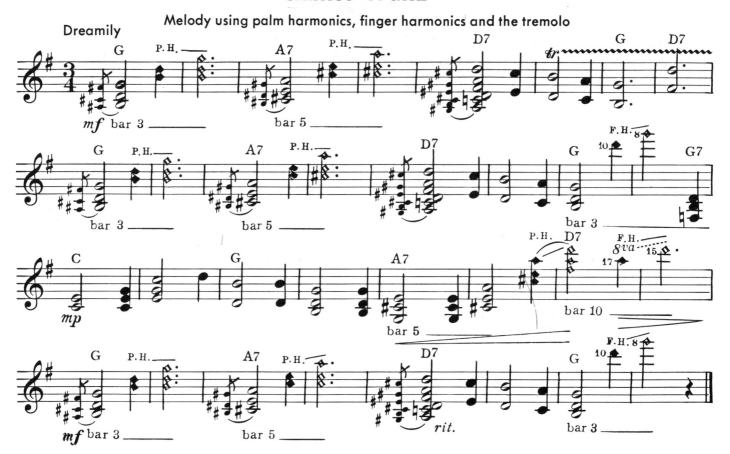

PALM HARMONICS ON LOWEST NOTE ONLY

A very beautiful effect is produced by playing thirds with the lower note a harmonic tone and the upper note a normal tone.

To produce this effect, let the wrist of the right hand dip downward allowing the palm to contact the strings twelve frets higher than where the steel is placed — then immediately after the thumb strikes the lower string for the harmonic tone, the palm is released and the thumb follows through striking the higher string as a normal tone — all of this is done quickly and within the time that it takes the thumb to strike across both strings. It is, of course, important that the palm contacts the string for the lower note to produce the harmonic tone, and is then released with a slight upward motion of the hand so that it does not contact the higher string to be played.

The example at the left shows that although the two notes are written in thirds, sixths are produced when the lower note only is played with the harmonic tone — the higher note sounding as written and the lower note sounding an octave higher than written or at an interval of a sixth above the melody note.

Isle of Dreams

Using palm harmonics on lower note only

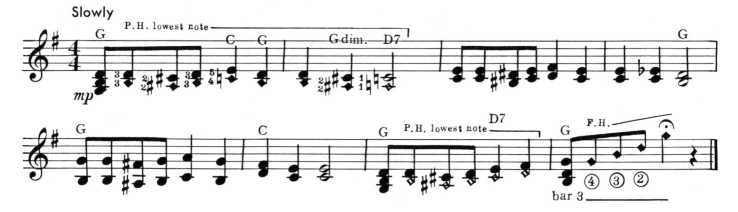

MOVABLE CHORD FORMATIONS

A careful study of the following movable formations will provide a short cut to the location of any chord.

A movable formation is one that can be shifted to any position on the fingerboard without changing the type of chord, the strings to be played or the relative position of the steel.

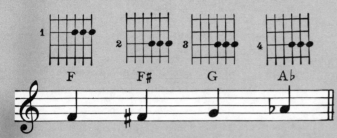

Thus if a major formation with the "root" as the highest note is shifted to another position on the fingerboard, it becomes another major chord with the "root" as the highest note.

The first chart shown here is the F chord, with the root as the highest note — moving the chord one fret higher makes an F# chord with F#, (the root) as the highest note.

The following charts show the most practical and most frequently used chord formations. Those marked I have the root as the highest note, those marked III have the third as the highest note, those marked V have the fifth as the highest note, and those marked VII have the seventh as the highest chord.

Only one chord of each formation is shown — move each formation to other frets on the fingerboard naming the chord and also the highest note of the chord.

MAJOR CHORD FORMATIONS

These formations will be easier to understand if you chart each one all the way up to the 5th fret and down to the lowest possible formation on separate manuscript paper — place the name of the chord under each chart as well as placing on the staff the highest or melody note of the chord.

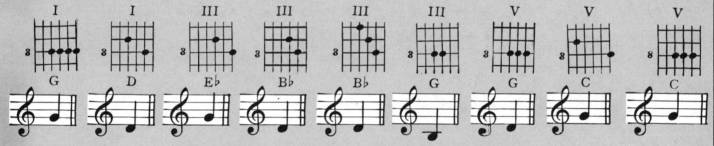

MINOR CHORD FORMATIONS

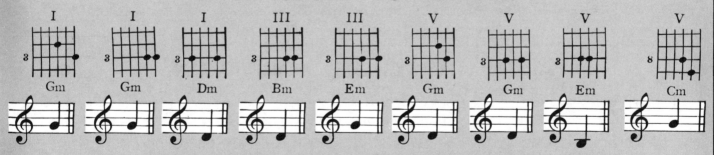

SEVENTH CHORD FORMATIONS

As any seventh chord contains the same notes as the major chord of the same name plus one additional note, the formations shown under MAJOR CHORD FORMATIONS can also be used as seventh chord formations.

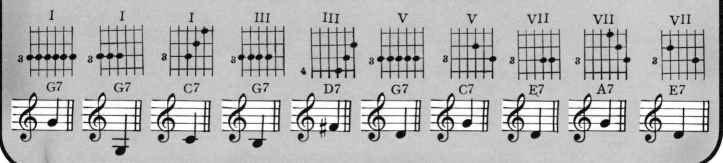

NINTH CHORD FORMATIONS

As any ninth chord contains the same notes as the seventh chord of the same name plus one additional note, the formations shown under SEVENTH CHORD FORMATIONS can also be used as ninth chords.

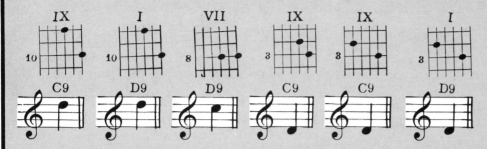

The examples here show several typical ninth formations frequently used — as only two notes are played, the same formation can be more than one ninth chord. As an example, if the notes E and D are played together, the chord can be used as C9 and also D9 — that is because C9 contains C E G B♭ D and D9 contains D F♯ A C E, both chords containing the two notes E and D. There are, of course, other ninth formations as any two intervals of the chord can be used — wherever possible the ninth interval of the root should be one of the two notes played to give the chord a distinct "ninth chord" sound.

DIMINISHED CHORD FORMATIONS

As explained before, each diminished chord has four different names and there are only three entirely different ones. The notes in the three diminished chords are as follows: 1. G♯ B D F, 2. F♯ A C E♭ and 3. C♯ E G B♭.

G♯, B, D, or F Dim CHORD

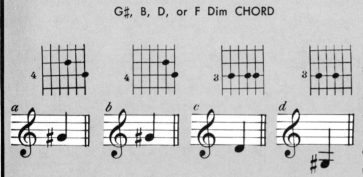

If any interval of a diminished chord is played on the first string another one can be added with a one fret slant on the third string as at *a* or with a one fret slant on the second string as at *b*.

A three note diminished chord is found by placing the 2nd, 3rd, and 5th strings at the bar position as charted at *c*. If the third string is used as the highest note of a diminished chord another interval can be added on the fifth string by using the bar position as at *d*.

Any diminished formation repeats itself three frets higher — as an example chart A shows two notes of the G♯ B D F diminished chord — moving the formation three frets higher again produces two notes of this same chord.

AUGMENTED CHORD FORMATIONS

Each augmented chord has three different names and there are only four entirely different ones. Any augmented formation repeats itself four frets higher on the fingerboard. As an example, the first chart shows the C aug. chord at the bar 4 position — moving the formation four frets higher to the bar 8 position also produces two intervals of the C aug. chord.

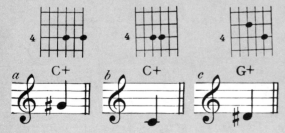

If any interval of an augmented chord is played on the first string another one can be added on the third string by using the bar position as at *a*.

If the third string is used as the highest note of an augmented chord another interval can be added on the fourth string by using the bar position as at *b*.

If the second string is used as the highest note of an augmented chord another interval can be added on the fourth string with a one fret slant as at *c*.

TWO NOTE CHORDS WITH MORE THAN ONE NAME

Two note combinations can be used for any chord that contains the two notes. The example here shows the two notes A and C — this combination can be used for F chord, D7 chord, Am chord, F7 chord, C dim chord and any other chord that contains the two notes A and C. Refer to the chart on page 48 and notice how all the chords mentioned as well as several others contain the two notes A and C.

MORE ABOUT TWO NOTE COMBINATIONS

Many two note combinations can be found at more than one position on the fingerboard — knowing where these formations are will often facilitate steel handling and make playing smoother.

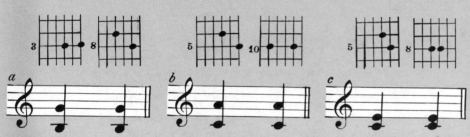

The example at *a* shows that combinations of "sixths" played on the first and third strings with the bar position can also be found five frets higher on the second and fourth strings using a one fret slant.

The example at *b* shows that "sixths" played with a one fret slant on the first and third strings can also be found five frets higher on the second and fifth strings using the bar position.

The example at *c* shows that "thirds" played with a one fret slant on the second and third strings can also be found three frets higher on the third and fourth strings using the bar position.

INDEX OF CHORDS

The following 15 pages show how to harmonize in the most practical way the most frequently used melody notes with all MAJOR, MINOR, SEVENTH, DIMINISHED, AUGMENTED, NINTH, MINOR SEVENTH, and MAJOR SIXTH CHORDS.

These chords can be used for reference whenever you are in doubt as to how any given note should be harmonized.

With the knowledge you have gained thus far by studying the previous pages you will need to refer to the index chords only occasionally.

CHORDS WITH MORE THAN THREE NOTES

In the charts more than three notes are often shown. Bear in mind, however, that in the three, four, five, and six string chords, it is permissible to play fewer strings to make progressions smoother, — always play the highest note as this is the melody — then add as many other strings as will make the arrangement smooth, progressive and musical.

Where more than one formation is shown for note, use the formation that makes progressions from the preceding or following chord smoother.

78

(C) C MAJOR FORMATIONS

The C Major chord contains the notes C E G — the following charts show how to harmonize the most frequently used melody notes with the C Major chord.

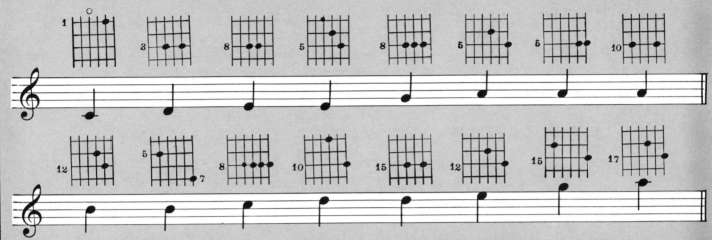

(Cm) C MINOR FORMATIONS

The C Minor chord contains the notes C E♭ G — the following charts show how to harmonize the most frequently used melody notes with the Cm chord.

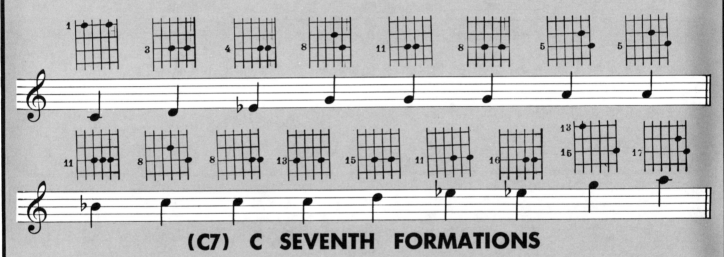

(C7) C SEVENTH FORMATIONS

The C Seventh chord contains the notes C E G B♭ — the following charts show how to harmonize the most frequently used melody notes with the C7 chord. As the C7 chord contains the same notes as the C chord plus one additional note, any of the formations listed under C Major chords can also be used when harmonizing with the C7 chord.

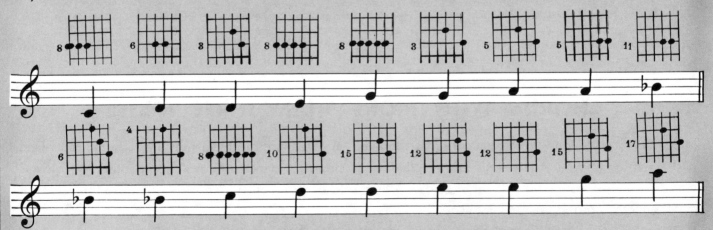

(C9) C Ninth-(Cm7) C Minor Seventh
(C6) C Major Sixth Formation

When harmonizing with the C9 chord use the formation listed under C7 — for Cm7 use the formations listed under Cm — for C6 use the formations listed under Am. The Am formations are on page 41.

(C# or Db) C# or Db Major Formations

C# chord contains the notes C# E# G# — Db chord contains the notes Db F Ab. These two chords are "enharmonic" — they sound and are played the same but are written differently — the following charts show how to harmonize the most frequently used melody notes with the C# or Db chord.

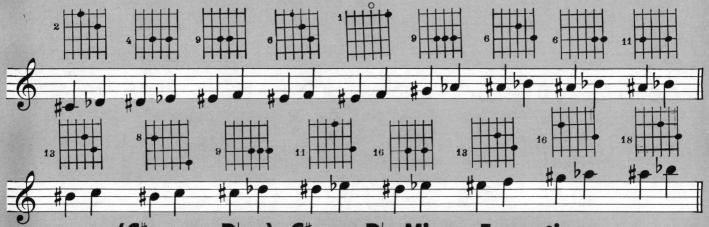

(C#m or Dbm) C# or Db Minor Formations

C#m chord contains the notes C# E G# — Dbm contains the notes Db Fb Ab. The following charts show how to harmonize the most frequently used melody notes with the C#m or Dbm chords.

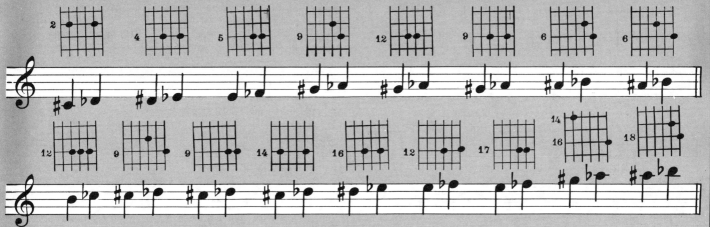

(C#7 or Db7) C# or Db Seventh Formations

The C#7 chord contains the notes C# E# G B — the Db7 chord contains the notes Db F Ab Cb. The following charts show how to harmonize the most frequently used melody notes with the C#7 or Db7 chords — for additional formations use those listed under C# or Db Major.

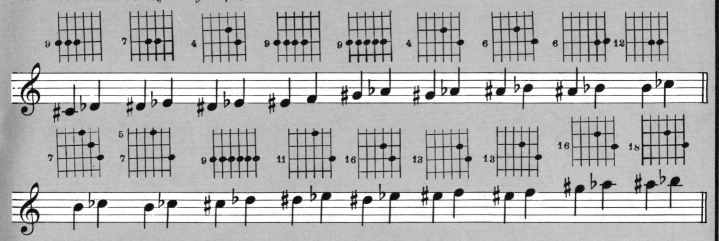

(C#9 or Db9) (C#m7 or Dbm7) (C#6 or Db6)

When harmonizing with the C#9 or Db9 chords use the formation listed under C#7 or Db7 — for C#m7 or Dbm7 use the formation listed under C#m or Dbm — for C#6 or Db6 use the formations listed under Bbm. The Bbm formations are on page 42.

(D) D MAJOR FORMATIONS

The D chord contains the notes D F♯ A — the following charts show how to harmonize the most frequently used melody notes with the D chord.

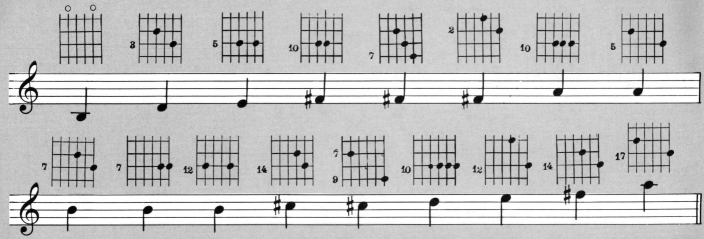

(Dm) D MINOR FORMATIONS

The Dm chord contains the notes D F A — the following charts show how to harmonize the most frequently used melody notes with the Dm chord.

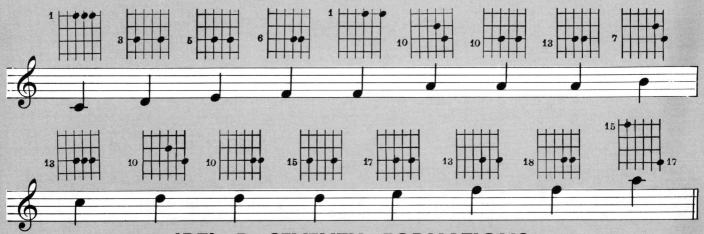

(D7) D SEVENTH FORMATIONS

The D7 chord contains the notes D F♯ A C — the following charts show how to harmonize the most frequently used melody notes with the D7 chord — for additional formations use those listed under D Major.

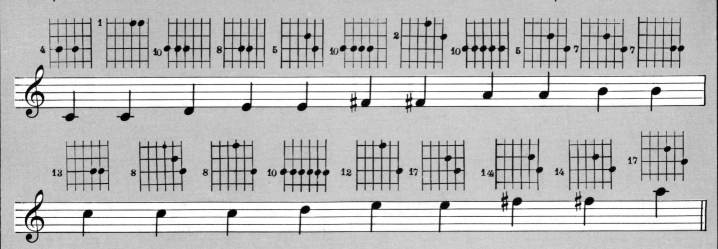

(D9)   (Dm7)   (D6)

When harmonizing with the D9 chord use the formations listed under D7 — for Dm7 use the formations listed under Dm — for D6 use the formations listed under Bm. The Bm formations are on page 43.

(E♭) E♭ MAJOR FORMATIONS

The E♭ chord contains the notes E♭ G B♭ — the following charts show how to harmonize the most frequently used melody notes with the E♭ chord. The following formations can also be used for the D♯ chord which contains the notes D♯ Fx A♯ — This chord is the enharmonic of E♭.

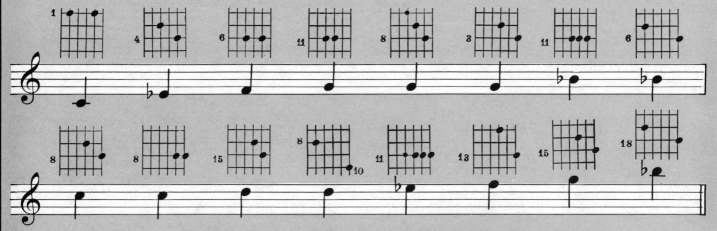

(E♭m) E♭ MINOR FORMATIONS

E♭m contains the notes E♭ G♭ B♭ — the following charts show how to harmonize the most frequently used melody notes with the E♭m chord — these formations can also be used for D♯m which contains the notes D♯ F♯ A

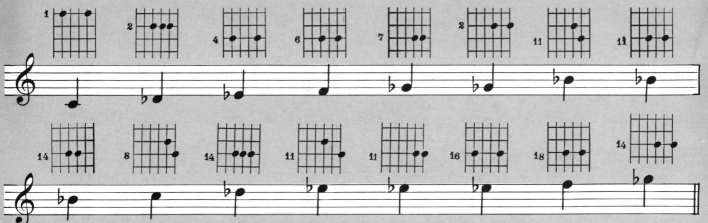

(E♭7) E♭ SEVENTH FORMATIONS

The E♭7 chord contains the notes E♭ G B♭ D♭ — the following formations can also be used to harmonize with the chord D♯7 which contains the notes D♯ Fx A♯ C♯ — for additonal formations use E♭ Major formations.

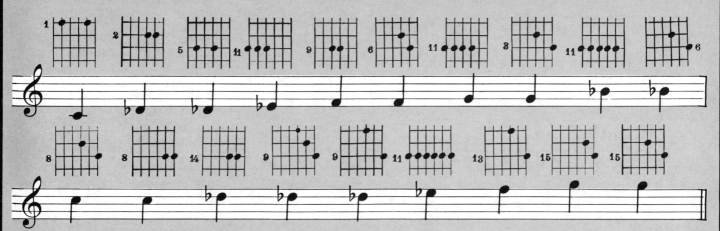

(E♭9 or D♯9) (E♭m7 or D♯m7) (E♭6 or D♯6)

When harmonizing with the E♭9 or D♯9 chords use the formations listed under E♭7 — for E♭m7 or D♯m7 use the formations listed under E♭m — for E♭6 or D♯6 use the formations listed under Cm. The Cm formations are on page 32.

(E) E MAJOR FORMATIONS

The E chord contains the notes E G♯ B — the following charts show how to harmonize the most frequently used melody notes with the E chord.

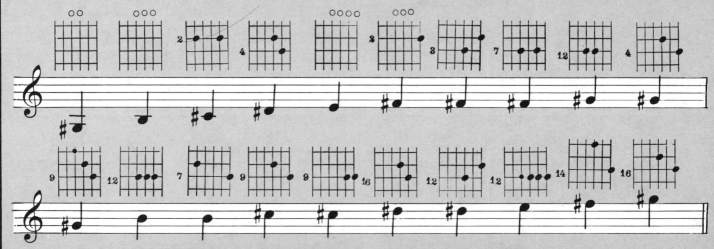

(Em) E MINOR FORMATIONS

The Em chord contains the notes E G B — the following charts show how to harmonize the most frequently used melody notes with the Em chord.

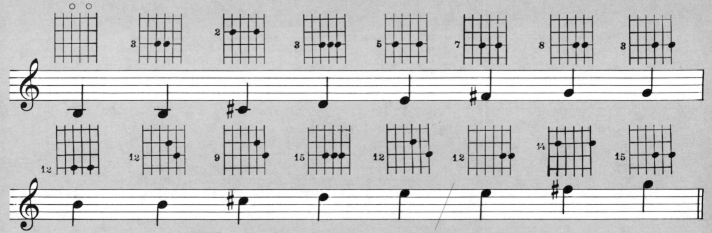

(E7) E SEVENTH FORMATIONS

The E7 chord contains the notes E G♯ B D — the following charts show how to harmonize the most frequently used melody notes with the E7 chord — for additional formations see E Major.

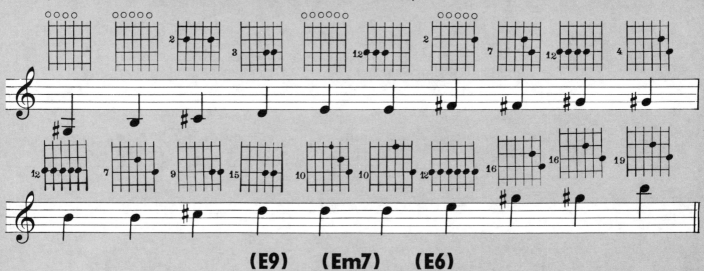

(E9) (Em7) (E6)

When harmonizing with the E9 chord use the formations listed under E7 — for Em7 use the formations listed under Em — for E6 use the formations listed under C♯m. The C♯m formations are on page 33.

(F) F MAJOR FORMATIONS

The F chord contains the notes F A C — the following formations show how to harmonize the most frequently used melody notes with the F chord.

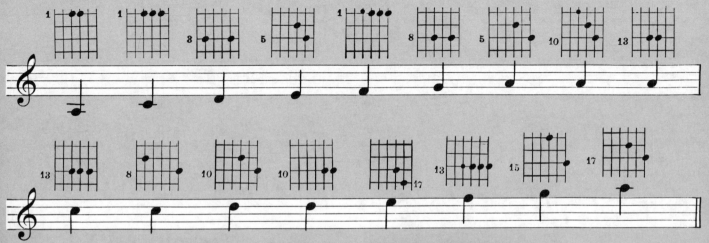

(Fm) MINOR FORMATIONS

The Fm chord contains the notes F Ab C — the following formations show how to harmonize the most frequently used melody notes with the Fm chord.

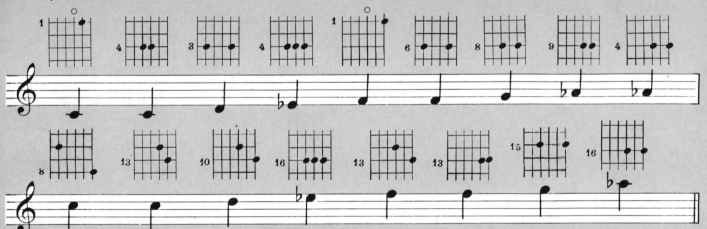

(F7) SEVENTH FORMATIONS

The F7 chord contains the notes F A C Eb — the following charts show how to harmonize the most frequently used melody notes with the F7 chord — for additional formations see F Major.

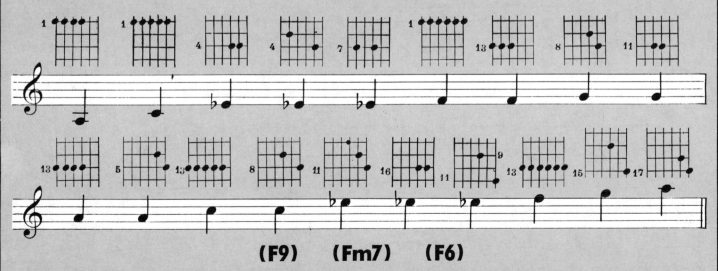

(F9)   (Fm7)   (F6)

When harmonizing with the F9 chord use the F7 formations — for Fm7 use the Fm formations — for F6 use the Dm formations. The Dm formations are on page 34.

84

(F♯ or G♭) F♯ or G♭ Major Formations

The F♯ chord contains the notes F♯ A♯ C♯ — the G♭ chord contains the notes G♭ B♭ D♭. These two chords are "enharmonic" — they sound the same but are written differently — the following charts show how to harmonize the most frequently used melody notes with the F♯ or G♭ chord.

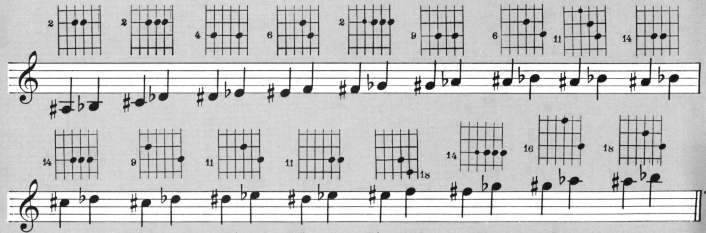

(F♯m or G♭m) F♯ or G♭ Minor Formations

The F♯ minor chord contains the notes F♯ A C♯. The G♭ chord contains the notes G♭ B♭♭ D♭. The following charts show how to harmonize the most frequently used melody notes with the F♯m or G♭m chords.

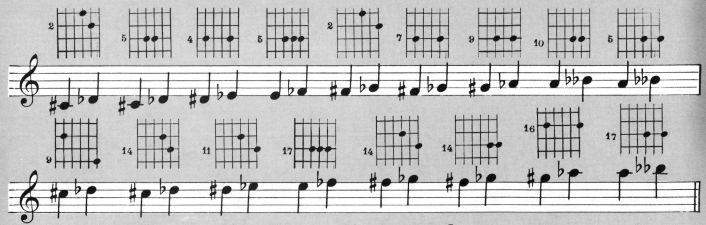

(F♯7 or G♭) F♯ or G♭ Seventh Formations

The F♯7 chord contains the notes F♯ A♯ C♯ E. The G♭7 chord contains the notes G♭ B♭ D♭ F♭. The following charts show how to harmonize the most frequently used melody notes with the F♯7 or G♭7 chords. For additional chord formations use those listed under F♯ or G♭ Major.

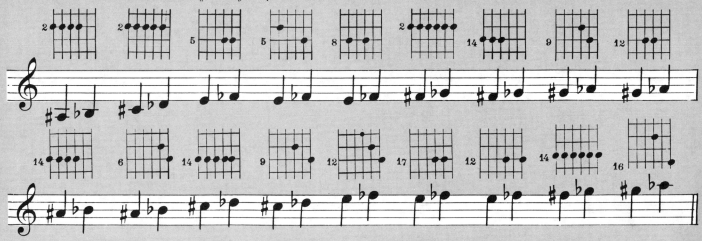

(F♯9 or G♭9) (F♯m7 or G♭m7) (F♯6 or G♭6)

When harmonizing with the F♯9 or G♭9 chords use the formations listed under F♯7 or G♭7. For F♯m7 or G♭m7 use the formations listed under F♯m or G♭m. For F♯6 or G♭6 use the formations listed under D♯m or E♭m. The D♯m or E♭m formations are on page 35.

85

(G) G MAJOR FORMATIONS

The G chord contains the notes G B D — the following charts show how to harmonize the most frequently used melody notes with the G chord.

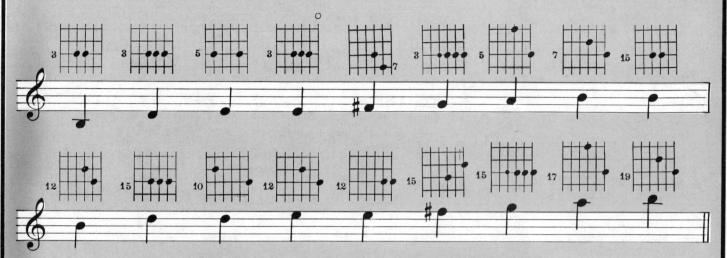

(Gm) G MINOR FORMATIONS

The Gm chord contains the note G B♭ D — the following charts show how to harmonize the most frequently used melody notes with the Gm chord.

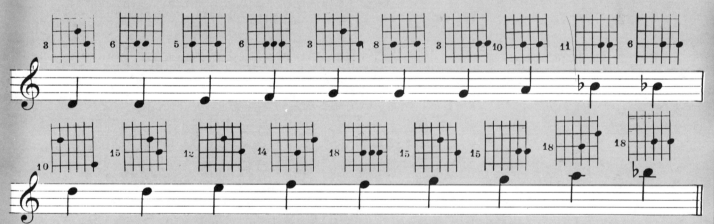

(G7) G SEVENTH FORMATIONS

The G7 chord contains the notes G B D F — the following charts show how to harmonize the most frequently used melody notes with the G7 chord. For additional formations use those listed under G Major.

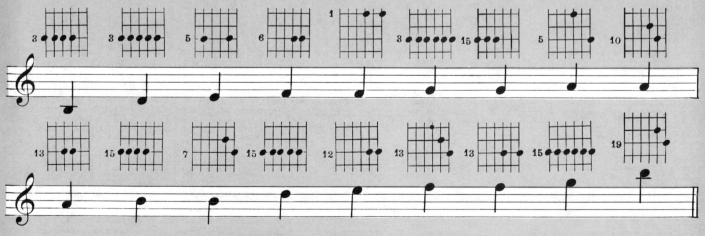

(G9)   (Gm7)   (G6)

When harmonizing with the G9 chord use the formations listed under G7 — for Gm7 use the formations listed under Gm — for G6 use the formations listed under Em. The Em formations are on page 36.

86

(Ab) Ab MAJOR FORMATIONS

The Ab chord contains the notes Ab C Eb — the following charts show how to harmonize the most frequently used melody notes with the Ab chord. The Ab chord is "enharmonic" with the G# Major chord which contains the notes G# B# D#.

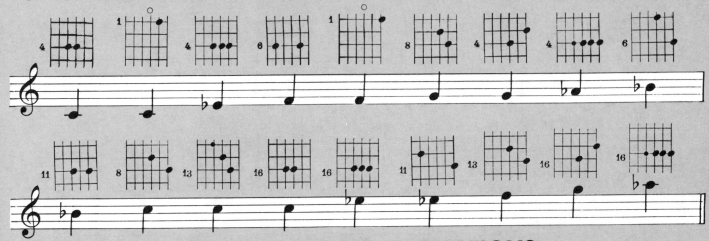

(Abm) Ab MINOR FORMATIONS

The Abm chord contains the notes Ab Cb Eb — the following charts show how to harmonize the most frequently used melody notes with the Abm chord. The Abm chord is "enharmonic" with G#m which contains the notes G# B D#.

(Ab7) Ab SEVENTH FORMATIONS

The Ab7 chord contains the notes Ab C Eb Gb — the following charts show how to harmonize the most frequently used melody notes with the Ab7 chord. For additional formations use those listed under Ab Major. These formations can also be used for G#7 which contains the notes G# B# D# F#.

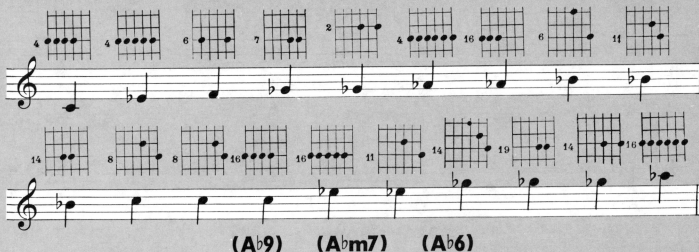

(Ab9)   (Abm7)   (Ab6)

When harmonizing the Ab9 chord use the formations listed under Ab7 — for the Abm7 chord use the Abm formations — for Ab6 use the formations listed under Fm. The Fm formations are on page 37.

(A) A MAJOR FORMATIONS

The A Major chord contains the notes A C♯ E — the following charts show how to harmonize the most frequently used melody notes with the A major chord.

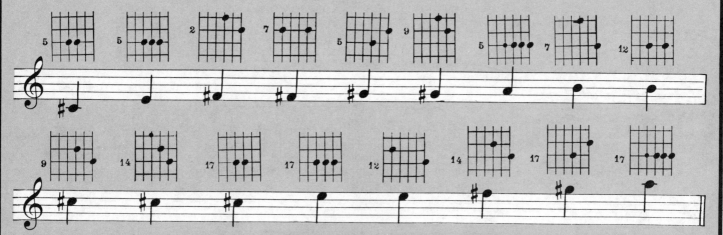

(Am) A MINOR FORMATIONS

The A minor chord contains the notes A C E — the following charts show how to harmonize the most frequently used melody notes with the A minor chord.

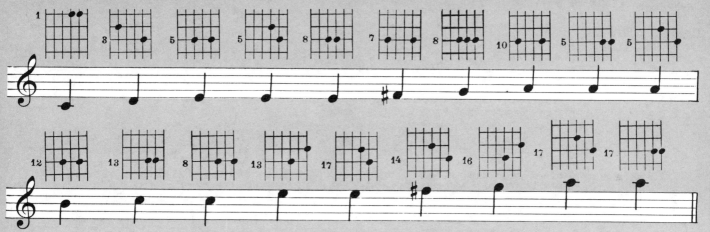

(A7) A SEVENTH FORMATIONS

The A seventh chord contains the notes A C♯ E G — the following charts show how to harmonize the most frequently used melody notes with the A seventh chord. For additional formations use those listed under A Major.

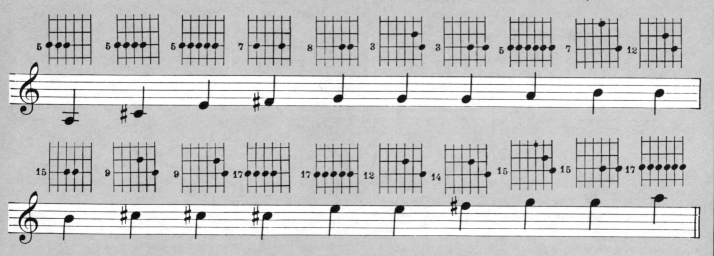

(A9) (Am7) (A6)

When harmonizing with the A9 chord use the formation listed under A7 — for the Am7 formations use those listed under Am — for A6 use the formations listed under F♯ Minor. The F♯m formations are on page 38.

(B♭) B♭ MAJOR FORMATIONS

The B♭ chord contains the notes B♭ D F — the following charts show how to harmonize the most frequently used melody notes with the B♭ Major chord.

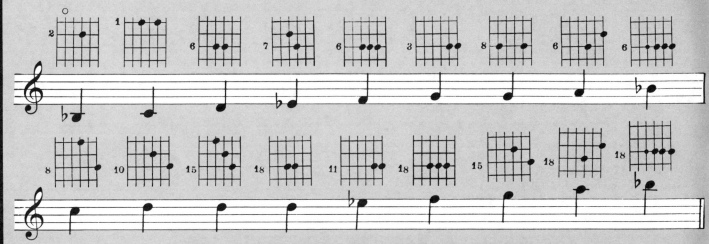

(B♭m) B♭ MINOR FORMATIONS

The B♭ minor chord contains the notes B♭ D♭ F — the following charts show how to harmonize the most frequently used melody notes with the B♭ minor chord.

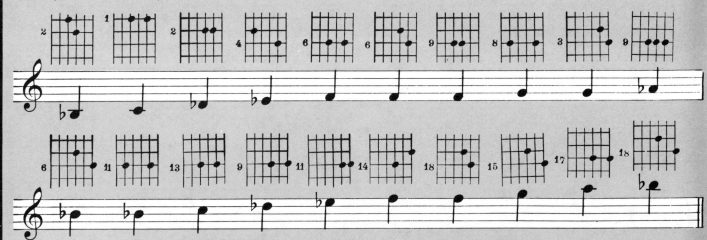

(B♭7) B♭ SEVENTH FORMATIONS

The B♭7 chord contains the notes B♭ D F A♭ — the following charts show how to harmonize the most frequently used melody notes with the B♭7 chord. For additional formations use those listed under B♭ Major.

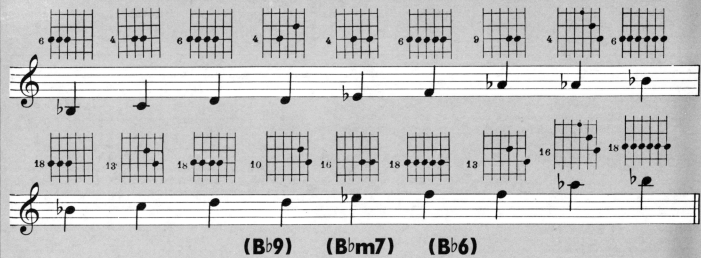

(B♭9)   (B♭m7)   (B♭6)

When harmonizing with the B♭9 chord use the formations listed under B♭7 — for B♭m7 use the formations listed under B♭m — for B♭6 use the formations listed under Gm. The Gm formations are on page 39.

89

(B) B MAJOR FORMATIONS

The B chord contains the notes B D♯ F♯ — the following charts show how to harmonize the most frequently used melody notes with the B chord.

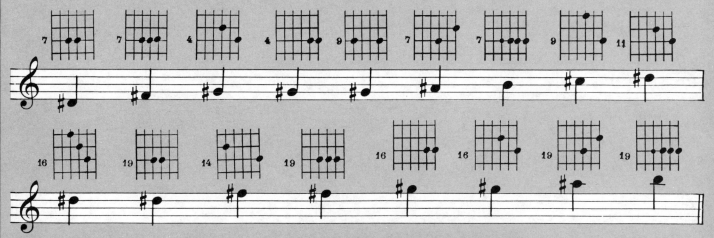

(Bm) B MINOR FORMATIONS

The Bm chord contains the notes B D F♯ — the following charts show how to harmonize the most frequently used melody notes with the Bm chord.

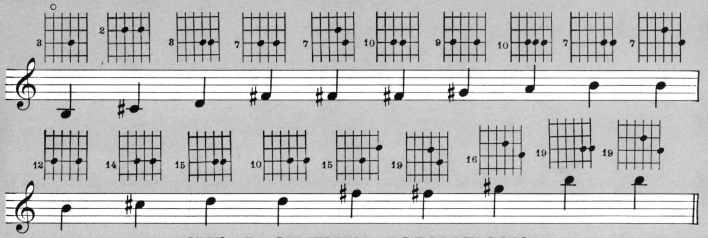

(B7) B SEVENTH FORMATIONS

The B7 chord contains the notes B D♯ F♯ A — the following charts show how to harmonize the most frequently used melody notes with the B7 chord. For additional formations use those listed under B Major.

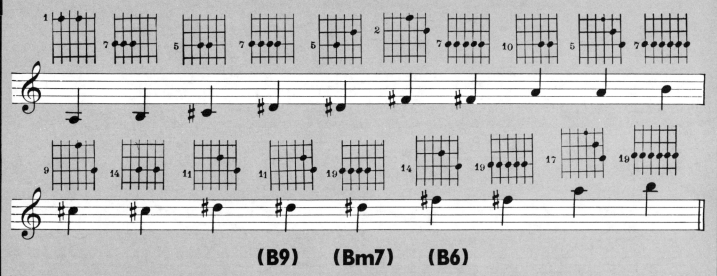

(B9) (Bm7) (B6)

When harmonizing with the B9 chord use the formations listed under B7 — for Bm7 use the formations listed under Bm — for B6 use the formations listed under G♯m or A♭m. The G♯m or A♭m formations are on page 40.

F# A C Eb DIMINISHED FORMATIONS

These formations can be used for F# dim, A dim, C dim, Eb dim — and also for the enharmonic chords of Gb dim and D# dim.

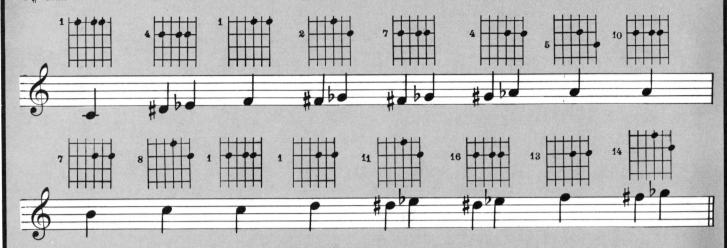

C# E G Bb DIMINISHED FORMATIONS

These formations can be used for C# dim, E dim, G dim, Bb dim — and also for the enharmonic chords, Db dim and A# dim.

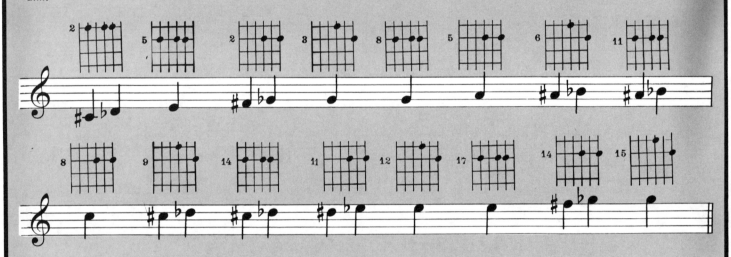

G# B D F DIMINISHED FORMATIONS

These formations can be used for G# dim, B dim, D dim, F dim — and also the enharmonic chords of Ab dim.

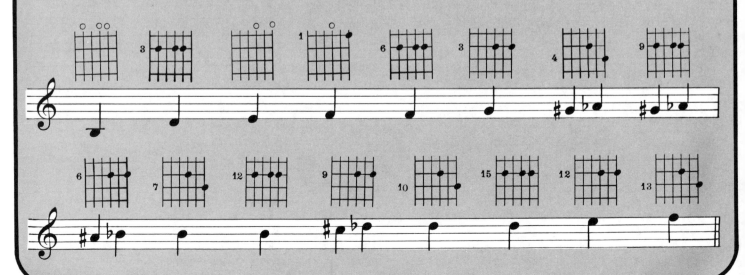

C E G♯ A♭ AUGMENTED FORMATIONS

These formations can be used for C+, E+, G♯+, and A♭+.

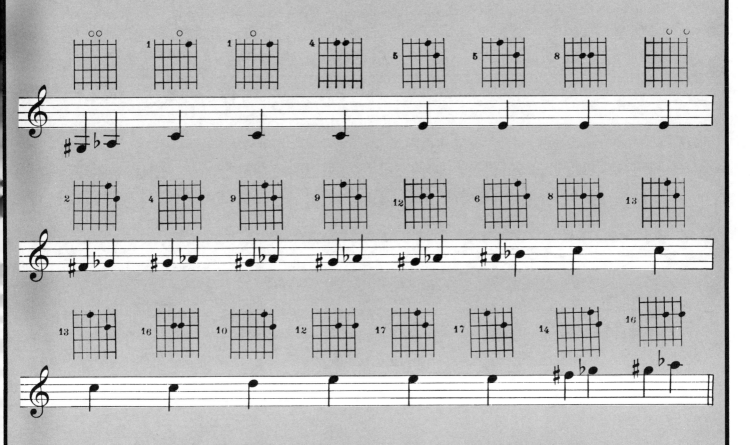

F A C♯ D♭ AUGMENTED FORMATIONS

These formations can be used for F+, A+, C♯+, and D♭+.

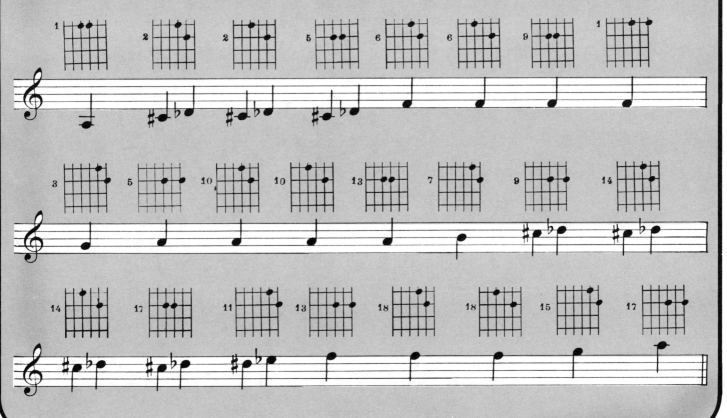

92

F♯ G♭ A♯ B♭ D AUGMENTED FORMATIONS

These formations can be used for D+, F♯+, A♯+, G♭+, and B♭+.

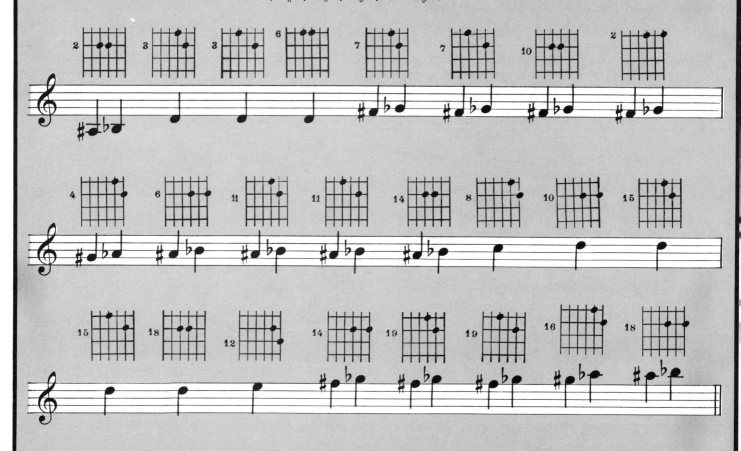

G B D♯ E♭ AUGMENTED FORMATIONS

These formations can be used for G+, B+, D♯+, and E♭+.

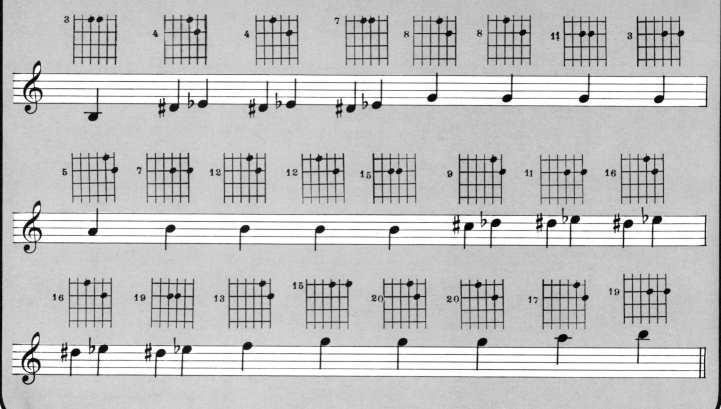

Picking the Strings

An excellent study in note reading and steel technique. Play the notes exactly as written without attempting to harmonize any of the melody notes.

Carefully analyze the rhythmic patterns — they are used quite frequently in modern playing.

When two or more notes are connected with a slur and a straight line ⌒ pick the first note or chord only and slide the steel to the others without picking the strings again.

Memorize this selection and practice it from time to time to develop steel handling.

CHORD SPELLING CHART

Showing the names of the notes in all of the most commonly used types of chords

Name of chord	Major	Minor	Augmented	Seventh	★ Diminished	Minor Sixth	Major Sixth	Minor Seventh	Major Seventh	Ninth
C	C E G	C Eb G	C E G#	C E G Bb	C Eb F# A	C Eb G A	C E G A	C Eb G Bb	C E G B	C E G Bb D
C#	C# E# G#	C# E G#	C# E# Gx	C# E# G# B	C# E G Bb	C# E G# A#	C# E# G# A#	C# E G# B	C# E# G# B#	C# E# G# B D#
Db	Db F Ab	Db Fb Ab	Db F A	Db F Ab Cb	Db E G Bb	Db Fb Ab Bb	Db F Ab Bb	Db Fb Ab Cb	Db F Ab C	Db F Ab Cb Eb
D	D F# A	D F A	D F# A#	D F# A C	D F G# B	D F A B	D F# A B	D F A C	D F# A C#	D F# A C E
D#	D# Fx A#	D# F# A#	D# Fx Ax	D# Fx A# C#	D# F# A C	D# F# A# B#	D# Fx A# B#	D# F# A# C#	D# Fx A# Cx	D# Fx A# C# E#
Eb	Eb G Bb	Eb Gb Bb	Eb G B	Eb G Bb Db	Eb F# A C	Eb Gb Bb C	Eb G Bb C	Eb Gb Bb Db	Eb G Bb D	Eb G Bb Db F
E	E G# B	E G B	E G# B#	E G# B D	E G Bb C#	E G B C#	E G# B C#	E G B D	E G# B D#	E G# B D F#
F	F A C	F Ab C	F A C#	F A C Eb	F G# B D	F Ab C D	F A C D	F Ab C Eb	F A C E	F A C Eb G
F#	F# A# C#	F# A C#	F# A# Cx	F# A# C# E	F# A C Eb	F# A C# D#	F# A# C# D#	F# A C# E	F# A# C# E#	F# A# C# E G#
Gb	Gb Bb Db	Gb Bbb Db	Gb Bb D	Gb Bb Db Fb	Gb A C Eb	Gb Bbb Db Eb	Gb Bb Db Eb	Gb Bbb Db Fb	Gb Bb Db F	Gb Bb Db Fb Ab
G	G B D	G Bb D	G B D#	G B D F	G Bb Db E	G Bb D E	G B D E	G Bb D F	G B D F#	G B D F A
G#	G# B# D#	G# B D#	G# B# Dx	G# B# D# F#	G# B D F	G# B D# E#	G# B# D# E#	G# B D# F#	G# B# D# Fx	G# B# D# F# A#
Ab	Ab C Eb	Ab Cb Eb	Ab C E	Ab C Eb Gb	Ab B D F	Ab Cb Eb F	Ab C Eb F	Ab Cb Eb Gb	Ab C Eb G	Ab C Eb Gb Bb
A	A C# E	A C E	A C# E#	A C# E G	A C Eb F#	A C E F#	A C# E F#	A C E G	A C# E G#	A C# E G B
A#	A# Cx E#	A# C# E#	A# Cx Ex	A# Cx E# G#	A# C# E G	A# C# E# Fx	A# Cx E# Fx	A# C# E# G#	A# Cx E# Gx	A# Cx E# G# B#
Bb	Bb D F	Bb Db F	Bb D F#	Bb D F Ab	Bb Db E G	Bb Db F G	Bb D F G	Bb Db F Ab	Bb D F A	Bb D F Ab C
B	B D# F#	B D F#	B D# Fx	B D# F# A	B D F G#	B D F# G#	B D# F# G#	B D F# A	B D# F# A#	B D# F# A C#

★ In giving the names of the notes in the diminished chords, enharmonic notes are often used to avoid too many double sharp and double flat signs.